This is a contemporary work of fiction. All characters, names, places and events are the product of the author's imagination or used fictitiously.

For queries, comments or feedback please use the following contact details:

Facebook: https://www.facebook.com/GeorgianaGrier/

Email: georgianagrier@labelleauboisdormant.co.uk

22 September 1326
Drodrecht
11:30 AM

As the French coast disappears behind her; Queen Isabella stands aboard the flagship of an invasion force made up of eight warships and mercenaries supplied by her son's father-in-law to-be, the Count of Hainault. She is looking towards the coast of England and recalling how, as a girl of twelve, she sailed the North Sea as the newly-married bride of Edward II of England. Now she is thirty-one, a queen, a mother, and an adulteress.

"You are the Queen now."

He could not have known what she was thinking, but as he so often did, Roger Mortimer was able to sense where Isabella's thoughts had gone when she was unaccountably silent.

There were so many memories to accommodate that she had spent the entire voyage from the Low Countries enslaved by the past, the distance to England not long enough to hold back the images that hurled themselves at her pained recollections.

The monotony of the sea should have soothed her, but she was on an errand of vengeance, one that called upon the legacy of her royal blood, the primacy of her womanhood, and the ancient rite of motherhood.

She sought the throne for her son and revenge for herself.

In order to be victorious, she would have to bring about the downfall of her husband, Edward II, the anointed king of England.

Success depended upon violating the laws of God, of king and of country. But failure would allow tyranny to triumph, and she could not permit that to happen.

Her besmirched honour demanded restitution, but her pride demanded revenge. No other way would it be assuaged.

"Yes," she replied. She was indeed queen now.

He was so close to her that, although their bodies did not touch, his physical presence once again cast its spell over her, owning her thoughts and intervening between her recollection of the past and her resolution for the future.

"I was so young. A mere girl, full of a girl's unfounded dreams. I could not have foreseen these events coming to pass," she whispered.

She was thirty-one years old now, the mother of the fourteen-year-old heir apparent, Prince Edward of Windsor. The years that had come and gone had taken their toll. But now, in charge of her destiny and armoured with the means to defeat her enemies, she felt young again. In Mortimer's arms, she was ageless.

"I was so young…so naive" she concluded.

The waves of the North Sea seemed eager to bring her to her destination as they lapped relentlessly against the hull of the ship, advancing like soldiers to a rhythm that struck her as martial.

She knew much of war: the battles with the Scots, the conflicts with the English barons, Edward's disputes with the King of France. They had made her a warrior.

Not all battles were fought with steeds and spears, however, and that child bride of twelve had not guessed that she would one day be engaged in a frightening and fierce war with a foe who could not be bested the way that an enemy in war could be defeated.

When she had crossed the English Channel as a bride in 1308, she had simply been *Isabella the Fair*, so named because of her beauty. Despite this, she held no arrogance, besides that which her birth right as a princess of France afforded her.

"'The beauty of beauties…in the kingdom, if not in all Europe,'" Mortimer quoted.

Isabella smiled at the memory of the words of Geoffrey of Paris. She had been buoyed by his flattery, and those words had carried her across the waters from England to France, instilling her with confidence that, even though she was leaving her native land and her father's royal court, she was bringing with her a pedigree of merit that would - she had childishly thought then - inspire her handsome Plantagenet husband to fall passionately in love with her, just as the bards of old had sung.

Her uncles had been with her then, full of reassurance that, although she was going to a country that was unknown to her, she would not be alone. Her Aunt Marguerite was the Queen Dowager of England, the second wife to the deceased Edward I. She had seemed content in her marriage with a Plantagenet, so there was no reason Isabella would not be content in hers.

Isabella sailed to England intent on being the cherished queen of Edward I's son. It was a match that, fiercely negotiated, had culminated in an uneasy alliance between the England and the France.

She had already been the wife of the king on her voyage to England, their wedding in *Boulogne*, a hazy memory.

That said she had enjoyed the elaborate ceremony that had celebrated her rise in prominence, and she had looked forward to a coronation that would be equally elaborate when the ship arrived on shore. Her uncles, Charles de Valois and Louis d'Evreux, were members of her royal entourage and would be present at her coronation, so she would not be alone.

Then Piers Gaveston had met them on shore. She had noticed the glances her uncles had exchanged as her husband had flung himself upon the man who had been granted special powers as regent, in his absence.

She had never seen such a display of affection between two men, but in her youthful inexperience, she had merely assumed that this was the custom among the English. It was not until she had seen the wedding presents that her father had bestowed upon Edward now adorning Piers Gaveston, who had dressed so opulently for her coronation that he was more resplendent than the king, that she began to perceive that something was not as it should have been.

She was too young, too inexperienced, to understand fully how much was amiss in her marriage.

Edward had sired children upon her; but it was not her company he sought in the middle of the night. It was Piers Gaveston's, the man he called his brother.

She had not known that such a dual nature was possible, that a man could both father children and give his love to a man.

The lessons she had learned as a young bride had been painfully taught and slowly absorbed. She had not been a willing student. But life was a merciless tutor.

23 September 1326
Paris, France
1:30 PM

The Archbishop of Norwich, William Airmyn is musing about the queen's departure.

William Airmyn sat in his temporary residence in Paris and sipped at the mulled wine that had just been prepared by his manservant. It was with great effort that he managed not to laugh aloud. By now, Queen Isabella would be on her way from Dordrecht to England to lay siege to her husband, King Edward II and bring him to his knees. William was to follow in a merchant ship in a couple of days. He should have felt unease at this act of treason, but he didn't.

He still smarted from the unjust treatment he had received at the hands of his monarch. Grimacing at the memory, he took another sip of his brew.

The relationship between England and France had been a complicated one for nearly a hundred years, the feudal obligations to the Duchy of Aquitaine being at the centre of it.

The king of England, Edward II was a mere vassal to the king of France, Charles IV, when it came to the Duchy of Aquitaine. This meant that he was under obligation to pay homage to Charles IV as his liege, something previous kings had successfully avoided doing.

Things had come to a head a little over two years ago,

when Charles IV had insisted without relent that Edward II personally pay homage to him.

William had no doubt that sneaky man knew exactly what he was doing, by demanding his due.

Why else would he have provoked an incident with Gascony shortly after - an incident that then justified his confiscation of the Duchy of Gascony and the County of Ponthieu, from Edward. Not even the surrender of Montpezet castle as a peace offering had appeased his ego.

Edward II's subsequent sorry attempt to raise an army to resist the French found no takers. With the English Channel controlled by French shipping, he did little to nothing to remedy the situation.

As the French entered Gascony in August 1324, the earl of Kent shut himself up in the fortress of La Réole without firing a shot.

William clenched his fists. If it had not been for the interception of the Archbishop of Dublin, who persuaded Kent to surrender and the subsequent diplomacy of the Bishops of Winchester (John Stratford) and Norwich (John Salmon), there would have been no peace in England, and a war would have started that even the papacy could not contain. Irritated by his own thoughts, William rose and stared out the window.

The French king and his sister played the game of thrones like master chess players. A truce was agreed in which Prince Edward of Windsor would pay homage on behalf of his father. Gascony was intrusted to the young English prince. The King had had no choice but to send his son and only heir to France to pay homage at Bois-de-Viencennes.

Once they arrived, however, Queen Isabella had used her son as a bargaining chip for the removal of the Despensers from her husband's court. The King, whom many (including William) had believed lacked a spine, refused. William shook his head in amazement.

Instead, he had declared the lands of Prince Edward to be forfeit, along with the lands of any whom he believe supported the Queen and her followers in Paris.

William had suddenly found himself lumped in with dubious characters, such as Roger Mortimer, the Earls of Kent and Richmond, Henry Beaumont, and the Bishop of Winchester, John Stratford.

Despite sending numerous missive to the royal court, it was to no avail. King Edward blamed William for the treaty and refused to restore the temporalities of Norwich. Not even the interception of Pope John XXII bore fruit. Instead, by June, William's brothers were arrested, all in an effort to force him to appear before the king's bench to answer charges of treason.

William had no choice but to flee to France and present his case and his full support to the Queen of England.

It had taken no time at all to accept his exile – since he had no intention of continuing to be in exile. Indeed, it had taken no time at all to start influencing the Queen to take action. Monarchs were prone to pride, and Queen Isabella and King Edward were no exception.

Soon, the invasion party would land on the soil of England, intent on disposing of Edward II. Soon, this entire ordeal would be over, and he would be headed back home.

William smiled, took another sip of his mulled wine, and continued to enjoy the view.

24 September 1326
The English coast
1:16 PM

The Suffolk port of Orwell ahead, the Queen is in deep conversation with her trusted advisor Roger Mortimer.

"The Despensers will be in flight, if they are not already," Mortimer said confidently, again exhibiting his uncanny ability to excavate the latent fears that lay buried beneath the layers of the Queen's troubled memories.

His body was close to her, his cloak brushing hers, and although she knew she should not have allowed this in plain sight, his leg pressed against hers, reminding her anew of the delight to be had from a man who knew how to please a woman, a man who had not shared himself or his love with a male rival who could not be vanquished in the manner of women because he possessed an allure that she could not match.

Roger's hand, possessive and reassuring, rested upon her shoulder. She should have forbidden him such familiarity, but she could not deny herself the comfort of his masculinity. Beneath his touch, she was again *Isabella the Fair*, a woman of renowned beauty, not the pathetic, ignored wife who could not keep her husband's affections.

She felt her body recline against his, and even though she ought not to have permitted it, she surrendered to the mesmerising power of his kiss as she felt his lips bury themselves in the indentation of her slender neck.

She hoped they were alone on the deck of the ship, but she knew it was unlikely. Everyone would see the proof of her adultery as they watched the knowing manner in which Baron Mortimer, revealed his intimate acquaintance with the person of the Queen.

Mortimer, a man who had mysteriously escaped death in the Tower following the revolt of the English barons and fled to the French court. A man with the devil's own luck.

She was playing with fire and once in England she knew it had to stop. She sighed deeply,

Would her marriage have been different had she not been introduced so quickly to the poison that Piers Gaveston had brought with him? She had endured his arrogance for four years, but she had not been alone in her resentment of the man her husband called his brother. The English lords despised him, as well.

Warwick, Lancaster, Hereford and Arundel had executed Edward's favourite four years after she'd become England's queen. She had thought then that her problems were solved. How foolish she had been.

"My Queen," Mortimer murmured, his words a rallying cry to her senses, reminding her of her status as queen even as her body declared him her ally, her beloved, her lord, her master. She was indeed a queen, but that meant that she was a woman, and it was the nature of her sex to seek strength and boldness.

Was she to blame because Edward had been so lacking in the attributes that Roger Mortimer possessed in abundance?

12

Even as the unkind thought flitted through her mind, she knew she was grasping at straws. Edward might prefer the company of men, but he was anything but effeminate. He had strong muscles from the manual work he so loved and was a towering presence. He should have found solace and whatever else he needed between *her* loins!

She would have forgiven him anything, supplied him with wenches if that was what he needed. But to be replaced by a man, her counsel belittled? She, the granddaughter of kings?

No, Edward was physically strong. His weakness lay elsewhere. She sighed.

She had been in England so long that she felt as if she were England's last hope. She knew that the English were in despair that their king had proven to be false. Weak in his dealings with his subjects, Edward II was gelded by his inability to rule with his father, Edward I's strength. His exclusive royal preference of the Despensers had only served to enrage his barons.

There had been a season when she had been able to mediate between the warring barons and her husband, but that was during the time of the first favourite, Gaveston. With his death and the rise of the Despensers, her influence had become so meagre as to be insignificant.

The Despensers.

It was strange to think that her life as queen had been more tolerable when her only rival was the vainglorious, sharp-tongued Piers Gaveston.

He had certainly been her enemy but had not claimed Edward as thoroughly as had his successor, Hugh Despenser the Younger.

The Despensers, the son as favourite and the father as mastermind, had made a mockery of her role as queen. They had persuaded Edward to confiscate her lands; they had convinced him to reduce her allowance until she felt as powerless as a servant.

She, doubly royal as the daughter of two monarchs in their own right – *Philip IV of France* and *Joan I of Navarre* - was the discarded queen, reduced to beggary and ignominy so humiliating that English clerics had pleaded with the Pope to intervene on the queen's behalf.

She had had no choice but to retaliate. In doing so, she had accumulated power. She was the leader of the rebellion, the protector of her son, Edward of Windsor, and no longer the impotent, scorned queen.

"The people will rise against the King," Mortimer

murmured, his lips warm against the skin of her temples.

"You *are* England, and they see you as their deliverer."

How did he do that? How did Roger Mortimer respond with his words to the thoughts inside her mind? Was it witchcraft? Had he come to possess her in mind, as well as in body? Did he know how utterly transformed she was by the alchemy of her remembered powerlessness and the surging force of Mortimer's passion...love?

Sometimes, the Queen wondered if all women were meant to be forever subjugated by love. Was this the real curse that had been inflicted upon Eve in the Garden of Eden, the pain of seeking a master in the man she loved?

Men did not understand how completely a woman's emotions simultaneously empowered and vanquished her.

She had borne a son, an heir to the throne, and for England, she had fulfilled her duty as the queen. She had supported the King as his wife, his consort, his advisor; it did not matter that their household was in England or that their works decided the fate of a nation. She had been born to be a queen; royal purple was in her bloodlines, and she had passed those bloodlines on to her son, who would rule as the third Edward in the Plantagenet line.

She was English in her goals. Her brother had only daughters, and the law of France did not permit women to ascend to the throne. Therefore, her son was the rightful heir, not only to the English crown, but also to the crown of France. She would be the means by which England and France would become a kingdom under the rule of her son.

She served the ends of the English by virtue of her French blood. And, through the alliance she had formalised with Philippa of Hainault, her son's dynastic ties would extend beyond England and France to the lucrative trade kingdoms of the Low Countries.

24 September 1326
Paris, France
1:47 PM

Charles IV, the king of France, is surrounded by his knights in his French court.

The minstrels were putting on a good show, but Charles's thoughts were firmly elsewhere. Soon his sister, Isabella would be reaching the coast of England.

He hadn't felt comfortable letting her lead the invasion by herself, but unless he wanted to launch the entire kingdom into a war with England, he needed to be crafty and let events play out.

Isabella was his last remaining sibling. His brothers, Louis X of France and Philip V of France, had died a couple of years prior. Whilst he had mourned their loss, he would mourn the loss of Isabella even more.

Despite her marriage to Edward II at the tender age of thirteen, she had been the family's little favourite. Her marriage had been a state decision, very much looked upon unfavourably by her three brothers. If the decision had been up to them, she would have stayed at home in France, where she belonged.

But the game of thrones was an inevitability in the House of Capet. It had been played for generations and would likely be played for generations to come. Their father, Philip IV, believed that true dominance came from having their bloodline on every throne in Europe, or at least as key figure in every courtroom. He had truly been *le Roi de fer* – the Iron King. Isabella had learnt about strategy from the moment of her birth.

Her marriage had cemented the uneasy peace between France and England, and the never-ending feud over Gascony and Flanders. Never had Charles imagined that she would subsequently fall for the heir she had married.

But now the breakdown of their marriage was playing

itself out on the court scene of Europe. Charles took a deep breath and let it out.

Only a mere eight years ago, the French court had been rocked by the *Tour de Nesle* scandal. It had led to the imprisonment of his own wife, Blanche of Burgundy, and that of his brother's wife, Margaret of Burgundy.

Charles was still not certain of the guilt of both wives and the knights who had been accused of leading them astray. He still remembered the execution, though.

Having been tortured, castrated, flayed alive and broken on a wheel, the men were still alive when they were hung. A gruesome business altogether.

The women were sequestered in Château Gaillard. Sentenced to life in prison, Margaret subsequently died mysteriously two years later; Charles, suspected it was his brother Louis's doing.

Blanche on the other hand survived in the underground hell of the castle dungeon until Charles had her released to a nunnery after his coronation. But freedom was too much for her, and she died within a year.

The events of the past were still very fresh in Charles' memory. Whilst the French court remained the court of love, a legacy left by Eleanor of Aquitaine, it had been disconcerting watching Mortimer's seduction of his sister.

The rumours had been so rampant that he had finally sent her to the Hainaults. It had only been sheer providence that had ensured that an alliance could be had with the duchy that was of benefit to both Isabella and the French Crown.

Summer had served to set the scene. In the name of protecting his nephew's right, Charles had occupied areas of Gascony from which he had earlier been withdrawing. Edward had of course retaliated, as expected. Charles smiled at no one in particular.

The destruction of Edward's fleet at Normandy some weeks before would ensure that the resistance to the invasion force his sister was leading was minimal. This was one of the reasons Charles had not hesitated to send his beloved sister out to war on her own.

That young English pup was about to find out that, in France, women were passionate about everything.

Passionate in love, but equally passionate in hate.

He only regretted not being able to be there to see the English whelp brought to his knees.

23 September 1326
Suffolk, England
1:55 PM

The port of Orwell ahead. Not all mercenaries and soldiers are as happy to be on their way to war.

Martin Dubois was standing quietly at the stern of the ship, watching his homeland slowly disappear into the horizon. He spat out the rancid tobacco he was chewing and mused at the folly of kings.

He knew he was only a lowly soldier, to be dispatched every which way at the whim of his superior and his sovereign, but frankly, this latest venture had him perplexed.

Hainault had enough problems as it was. Why the Count would ever agree to send armed men to support that French shrew, Queen Isabella, was beyond him.

There was not a single peasant who had not heard the story of debauchery that had played out in France. Hadn't the queen left her husband and king to take a lover in Paris? It was common knowledge that the French were debauched, but to support their bid to allow a woman to rebel against her monarch was lunacy. He had no wish to die for the likes of that.

This was his last mercenary voyage. He hoped England would not be his final resting place.

He caressed the pommel of his blade, praying it would stay true to him and bring him safely home. If he was lucky,

Marie Dubois, the local tavern girl, would still be free and waiting for him.

They had not yet exchanged any words to that end, but he felt certain that, once he raised enough of a dowry on this mission, his proposal would be looked favourably upon.

That Marie, she was a good girl…with nice childbearing hips. Martin smiled to himself. He was looking forward to the day he would be able to explore those creamy hips.

His grip tightened around his sword. He just had to make sure he survived this damned war…with all his limbs intact.

23 September 1326
Suffolk, England
2:42 PM

On the approach to the port of Orwell, Queen Isabella's destiny awaits her.

Isabella chided herself for the amount of time she had spent daydreaming and reminiscing about the past. What was done was done. Any moment now, she was to set foot on English soil. Her army awaited her.

Only the future mattered. Securing it for her son and his

heir against Edward's future follies came first.

Her allies had gathered around her, ninety-five ships with around a thousand men, not including the mercenaries recruited in Germany and Hainault by the brother of Count William of Hainault.

But power called forth ruthlessness. She could not achieve her goals if she appeased the Despensers, and Edward would not consent to any negotiations that took away his favourite or overruled the power of the Despensers. Within the hidden marrow of her body, she knew that the means for victory required bloodletting and violence.

She was bringing a mighty and growing force to the shores of England so that the English king could be overthrown. Deposed kings needed to be disposed of, or they became magnets for the dissatisfied, power-seekers, and the dispossessed. A living former king was a threat. She knew this, but refused to acknowledge what she might need to do to safeguard her son's future.

As long as she was on board the ship, with the boundary of the water separating her from shore, she did not have to face what lay ahead, or the violence that was incumbent of an invading army. The water was her solace; the endless ripples of the waves that brought her to her destiny seemed calm and resolute now. She would arrive in England when the sea decided to bring her to shore, and until then, she was still innocent of whatever sins and crimes she was required to commit.

"The king keeps a knife in his *chausses*; he intends to kill you with it," Mortimer whispered, his lips hot and searching against the soft, supple skin of her cheek. She had been so lost in her musing that she had almost forgot he was there. Discreetly she pushed him gently away…she could not have him display his affection openly. She was still the queen of England. She gazed down into her goblet.

How had they come to this point? Isabella did not know. How had she come to be here, on a ship financed with the money from the dowry given by her future daughter-in-law, with the intent of overthrowing the king, her husband? How had the French bride turned into the English invader? How had the queen been driven back to France, and how had she then been made unwelcome at her brother's court? How had this happened?

There was still time to bring the king to his senses, to dispose of the hated Despensers and convince Edward that he could not continue as he had been. He had incurred the enmity of his lords and the disapproval of the Holy Church. Perhaps he could be convinced that this was the path to ruin, that by driving away his wedded wife in favour of a hated favourite, he jeopardised the very throne that his ancestors had occupied with such resolution. Perhaps there was still time, before the North Sea waters brought her to her destiny and Edward's doom.

"Your Grace." The ship's captain approached her and bowed, taking care to avert his eyes from the sight of Roger Mortimer's hand upon her skin, his fingers below the jewels that encircled her neck and above the pearl-studded neckline of her gown.

"We approach England. We will disembark soon."

It was too late. She closed her eyes, succumbing to the intoxicating pleasure of Mortimer's knowing touch and her own fate.

The Queen of England had returned.

23 September 1326
London, England
3:52 PM

Residential quarters of the Tower of London.

The English palace is secure, and Edward feels safe here, confident that his efforts will thwart his wayward Queen's ambitions. He has made preparations for the invasion, and the Despensers have assured him that his efforts are exactly what a strong king should do, even if that means repudiating his adulterous wife and his disobedient son. But what is easy for the Despensers, whose power depends upon the authority of the king, is not so simple for the king himself, who is husband and father to the two people who are now his enemies.

Edward II surveyed his surroundings with satisfaction. "My father himself fortified this palace," he declared. "No one knew more about fortifying a castle than him. It cost him twenty-one thousand pounds, and it took him a decade, but look at the results."

Hugh Despenser the Elder, who had served King Edward I well enough to have been made a baron through the monarch's bounty, nodded his appreciation of the late king's acumen in the art of fortifications.

Edward I had excelled in so many areas that it was almost tedious to recount them. He had been a paragon of kingship, to be sure, but it was Edward II who had made Despenser the Elder the earl of Winchester, and such a gift countermanded any obeisance to the dead Plantagenet.

Hugh Despenser the Younger nodded.

"Did not your royal grandfather also restore the Tower to

25

magnificence?"

Eagerly, Edward launched upon this topic. "He did; yes, he did. My grandfather was a man of refinement, and he wished to reside in the comfort that the royal family had a right to enjoy.

"Yes," Edward repeated, warming to the subject of construction, a favourite of his.

"King Henry III knew what his father had endured at the hands of the arrogant barons, and he wanted to ensure that his family would be safe from such insubordination. I wish I had known him," Edward said wistfully. "We should have had much to talk about. What a sublime joy it would have been to converse as the building of Westminster Abbey began. I should have liked to have been part of that."

"Your father would not have permitted it," Hugh the Younger reminded Edward.

The King frowned. His father had never approved of what he regarded as his son's rustic preferences. Edward I revelled in war and did not understand how a son of his body and blood could find more pleasure in thatching a roof than in the manly arts.

It had been futile to point out that building was a useful art and that surely the kingdom needed roofs more than it needed additional corpses.

But the sons of kings did not build bricks, or dig in the dirt, or engage in the rough plebeian labour of the commons. Not for the first time, Edward wondered what his life would have been like had he not been born to the purple.

What if he had been the son of a farmer? It would have been his duty to tend to the fields and maintain his humble cottage. Edward mused upon this idyllic vision. He would have been happy to have been born into that state, he thought.

The flickering candlelight, captured by the facets of the jewels gleaming around Hugh the Younger's neck, caught Edward's gaze. The idyll faded. Farmers could not afford to give their favourites such gifts, and it gave Edward great pleasure to bestow luxurious presents upon those around him, but particularly upon Hugh, who was so loyal and constant, and who provided such comfort to sustain him as he endured the fiendish behaviour of his turncoat queen.

"We will be safe here," Edward promised, abandoning the discussion of his father's displeasure as if it had not taken place. "There is no more secure palace in all of England."

"And yet," commented Hugh the Elder, "Mortimer escaped."

Edward slammed his goblet down; droplets of wine spilled out upon the stately oaken table around which the three men sat.

"Mortimer was aided in his escape by my false queen!" he exclaimed. "The palace, and the prison, too, are inviolate. We are safe here. You forget that I am the king!"

"Sire, I never forget that you are the king," Hugh the Elder replied.

"Of course not. And England will not forget that you are the king," Hugh the Younger added quickly, giving his father a dark, warning glance. "The Queen is false, as you say. She has soiled the royal bed of England with her adultery. She has lured your son from his filial duty with her lies. You are the King, sire. You must behave as a king would, and despite your tender heart and your affection for the Queen and your son, Edward of Windsor, you must take action against them."

"I have ships waiting upon the shoreline. I have ordered two thousand men to the coast to guard against the queen's invasion," Edward flung back. "Are two thousand men so paltry a defence? I have a force of sixteen hundred in Normandy to divert the queen and her troops. I am the King; I know how to protect my realm."

"Yes, yes," Hugh the Younger said soothingly, reaching out his hand to clasp the King's wrist and then to caress the sleeve of the King's robe. "But in order to be strong, must not the King steel his heart against the weakness of affection?"

Hugh the Younger's touch was hypnotic and reassuring. He knew how to sooth the monarch, like no other. They were alone, except for Hugh the Elder, who was privy to the bond that his son and the king shared. Neither of them paid attention to the grimace Hugh the Elder made as he diverted his gaze.

23 September 1326
London, Aldgate
The House of Minoret Sisters
4:34 PM

The Dowager Badlesmere, Margaret de Clare, turned towards the abbess, Alice de Sherstede, and nodded. Today was a joyous day indeed. It had been almost five years since the incident that had led to the imprisonment of her and her children in the Tower of London. But the affront to her family was something she had no intention of forgetting, neither that nor the execution of her husband.

Plastering on a more neutral expression, she addressed the

abbess. "These events are troubling, to say the least, Your Holiness."

"To marshal an army and set forth to dethrone one's king and husband is surely treasonous," the abbess muttered.

"Without a doubt."

"I find myself in a most uncomfortable situation. The Queen is our most valued patroness, but her actions go against God and Country," the abbess continued to lament.

"The most prudent thing to do is surely to pray for their immortal souls," Margaret offered in a pious voice.

"You are very right, my dear. We shall order four days of continuous prayer for the king and queen," the abbess replied with a look of relief. She swiftly turned and walked away with renewed purpose.

Margaret strolled through the garden of the abbey, a small smile playing on her lips. Despite Edward II's provision of a stipend and the restoration of a significant portion of her late husband's manors, she felt no loyalty to him.

She might not be adept at the game of thrones, but she had the self-awareness to know when she had been manipulated. The memory of that event at Leeds was burned into her mind. Her hands clenched.

She remembered it as if it were yesterday. She had still

been reeling from her abduction and the assault on her servants in Hertfordshire two years prior to the event, when the king and his wife had made their move.

Never again did she have any intention of finding herself in such a vulnerable position as to let a known enemy get that close to her person. If circumstances had been otherwise, she still would not have wanted to extend her hospitality to that upstart, Isabella.

That the queen sought shelter at Leeds Castle, whilst her husband and lord was away, would have seemed suspicious to anyone. Margaret did not regret turning her away that day; she only regretted not having used more lethal force. The subsequent war because of her refusal, her imprisonment in the Tower, and the beheading of her husband had done nothing to mellow her feelings. It had taught her how to hide them, though.

Before she was fully immersed in her memory, she heard running footsteps. It was her twelve-year-old son, Giles.

"Mother! Mother! Is it true? Has the queen declared war on the king with the intent to march an army to the gates of London?" The words tumbled out of his mouth in a rush.

"Yes, my son. But do not let that bother you. The game of thrones will be yours to play sometime in the future. But today, all you need be is my beautiful knight," she whispered as she embraced him tightly.

Giles squirmed at the affectionate display as he tried to pull loose. His mother laughed out loud and ruffled his hair. Together, they made for the main building in a jovial frame of mind.

25 September 1326
London, England
9:18 AM

Residential quarters of the Tower of London. Edward II is still in turmoil. The Despensers work hard to persuade him to act against his rebellious family.

"What should I do?" Edward whispered. He had yet again asked for prayers from the Dominican friars of Oxford on behalf of himself and his realm, but had omitted his beloved queen and son. Now, doubt plagued him.

Could he really go to war against those he held dearest in his heart? He looked up at Hugh Despenser the Younger and his father standing to the side. It was always easier to follow the advice of the Despensers. They cared for him and for his welfare.

They were not zealous to weaken his authority, as the English barons were.

They did not campaign against him with the French king, as his wife did.

They had not forgotten their duty to him, as his son had done.

He had not had such advisors since Piers Gaveston had been taken from him. Piers, too, had recognised his enemies for what they were: scheming, covetous vultures who sought their advancement at the expense of the throne.

Why could the barons not have allowed Piers to live?

Warwick had been the one who sentenced Piers to death. But God had judged him for his crimes; Warwick had died the following year.

Yet Edward had been lonely after Piers' death. Isabella had been different then, a solace for him. They had gotten on better then; she had not sought to thwart him. She had been occupied, as a woman should be, with breeding. Four children alive, two of them sons.

That was not as many children as his father had sired, but two sons were ample security for the monarchy. Had the Isabella been dutiful as a wife should be, it would not have been necessary for him to chastise her eight years ago by placing his niece, Eleanor de Clare, Hugh the Younger's wife, in the household to monitor her correspondence, as she was communicating with her brother.

That her brother was the king of France was irrelevant; she had married an English king, and France was the enemy.

Edward had been forced to take the Isabella's lands from her and give them to the Despensers because his wife could not be entrusted with their safekeeping.

She had failed in her duties as a wife and a queen.

She had sought power beyond her sex.

It was not for frail womanhood to have ambitions beyond what God had ordained for a woman to expect.

"What must I do?" he asked again.

"You must outlaw them," Hugh the Elder responded. He answered so seamlessly that one might have thought that father and son had already discussed the matter, but that was absurd because their loyalty, Edward knew, was to him first.

"The Queen has transgressed in her duty to you, and she has violated the obligations of motherhood. The Church is clear on a woman's duty, and Queen Isabella has sinned. She has taken a lover; what if she should conceive a child by Mortimer? To have a bastard foisted upon the royal lineage would bring shame to the House of Plantagenet. Your royal father would never have countenanced such a gross abuse of his royal person."

Hugh the Elder was right; he always was, of course. Once again, Edward realised how fortunate he was to have such sage counsel from someone whose abiding concern was not for privilege or beneficence, but for Edward's own wellbeing.

"Yes," Edward agreed emphatically. "He would not have endured it. They shall be outlawed! How dare she think that she can turn my son against me and violate my crown? I am anointed by God, and I will not be gainsaid on this! They are outlawed herewith!"

Hugh the Elder bowed his head in obedience.

"It shall be as Your Grace orders," he said.

"England is fortunate to be ruled by so wise a king, one who places his duty before his heart," Hugh the Younger agreed. His fingers moved from the fabric of the King's sleeve to the flesh underneath.

"Fortunate indeed."

25 September 1326
London, England
9:55 AM

Servants' quarters of the Tower of London.

Anne Herman, one of the chambermaids of the Tower, scurried from the alcove where she had been hiding. Her heart beating with fear because of what she had just overheard.

England was at war!

She cared not for the machinations of lords and ladies, but it had sounded as if the war could be of such a scale that men would be recruited from London itself to oppose the queen. She bit her lower lip.

She had both a brother and a lover that she did not want to see anywhere near this coming war. She would have to warn them to leave the city and hide out in the countryside. It was not unheard of for a monarch to forcibly recruit men to join his army on penalty of death.

Sheer terror overwhelmed her. The memory of her father's conscription and later death was still fresh in her mind. She took some deep breaths to calm herself. There was still time.

"Well, what have we here?" asked a masculine voice behind her. It belonged to one of those stupid lords who was under the impression that she craved his attentions. In reality, she did what she had to do to put aside the money she needed for her to leave her demeaning drudgery of a life.

"My Lord Glaston," she murmured, and curtsied in her

woollen dress. She had long since stopped wondering why these men would seek the company of the likes of her, when they had beautiful, perfumed women at their beck and call.

"Miss Anne, how fortuitous to come upon you," he said with a knowing gleam in his eyes. He let his hand slowly slide across her face down to her ample bosom.

"How may I be of service, sir?" she replied with a forced smile.

Lord Glaston was beyond noticing subtle facial expressions, and frankly, sometimes he wanted his prey to resist.

"Be a good wench and come over here. I need to quench the thirst of my groin," he muttered as he dragged her into the nearest alcove.

They both knew the likelihood of any other person besides a servant stumbling upon them was very low. This was the very reason Lord Glaston liked roaming around the servants' quarters.

Soon, Anne found herself bent over, her skirts draped over her back. Lord Glaston took his time as he filled her repeatedly with his hard member.

She endured this as she had so many times before, even making little noises to feed into his fantasy, but her thoughts were firmly on the money he would be giving her after he finished and what the best way was to get her loved ones out of the city.

As he emptied himself, she was grateful that she regularly went to Madame Rankin to replenish her potion against carrying a babe.

She smiled as he gave her the money. Deep down, she marvelled at what disgusting, debauched monsters the English noblemen were.

She soon pulled down her skirt and scurried off to help her brother and lover escape the city.

25 September 1326
Aboard a ship docked at Orwell in Suffolk England
4:03 PM

The fourteen-year-old Edward of Windsor awaits the start of England's invasion, aware of the fact that whatever his mother and the powerful Baron Roger Mortimer decide to do will be done in the name of Edward of Windsor, the future king. Where does his duty lie? With his father, whose reign has been one of upheaval and dissension? With his mother, who has returned with an army financed by the dowry of the young woman Edward is contracted to wed? With England, the kingdom he will rule? He is very young and not yet a man, although he has the Plantagenet height and air of command. How can he claim his destiny when he is still under the authority of two parents who are in opposition to one another?

"Your Grace, we have docked in England."

Edward of Windsor nodded, but said nothing. What was there to say? His father had sent him to France to do homage for the English king's French lands, Guyenne, Gascony, and Ponthieu. Or had the Despensers sent him to France?

He had done as he was bidden, a dutiful son to two parents whose marriage was, he knew, in a state of siege because of the Despensers who wielded such power over the throne.

Once in France, he had learned that his homage was a mere ruse. He had been summoned from France not to solve the dilemma of the dispute over Edward II's French possessions, but to solve a greater problem, that of the king himself and his inability to reign.

His uncle, the earl of Kent, Edmund of Woodstock, was half-brother to the king and had been loyal until the Despensers had driven him to France, where he had joined the growing number of mutinous English who sought restitution of their rights.

"Your Grace."

Edmund had not left the ship's cabin, where Edward of Windsor, heir apparent to the throne, was lodged in what minimal state could be provided.

"We've arrived in England."

"Yes, I heard you," Edward replied impatiently. Edmund was only eleven years Edward's senior, with the result that they were more like cousins than uncle and nephew, yet Edmund was a man grown. He could not possibly understand the quandary in which Edward found himself.

For Edmund, the disloyalty to the King came about after years of support. He had forgiven his half-brother for failing to honour the intentions of their father, Edward I, to bestow grants of land upon the son of his second marriage.

The favourite Piers Gaveston, who had been executed before the birth of Edward of Windsor, had benefitted from that omission. But Edmund's earldom had subsequently come from his half-brother, and he had been content.

Edward knew that his uncle had served his father well, both in diplomacy and in arms. But the Despensers had proven to be more than even a loyal half-brother could endure or ignore.

"What was my grandfather like?" Edward queried.

Edmund had not expected the question.

"I was but a boy of six when he died. My memories are those of a child," he replied, dodging the question.

"You must remember something," Edward insisted. "I have no recollection of him; I was not yet born. I know the legend, but the man is a stranger to me."

"He was a giant to me," Edmund returned. "They called him Longshanks, as you know, for his height. He had a great temper. He was often away at war. I suppose I was a trifle fearful of him, as young children are of a parent who is masterful. He was a king. My notions of what a king ought to be are formed in his image. He fulfilled his obligations, as a king ought to do."

"Yes, but he was your father. What did you think of him as a son?"

Edmund did not know how to explain to this youth that a young boy did not perceive his father in abstract terms. He had been a mere child, the product of the king's union with his second wife, and no threat to the inheritance, no dynastic ingredient to the lineage.

"He was a giant," Edmund repeated. "I respected him and obeyed him as a dutiful son ought to do. But . . . his eyelid drooped," Edmund recalled, ashamed of the memory that remained after all these years. "His left eyelid. His eye

41

seemed to forever be half-closed. It frightened me. Silly, the things that a child notices."

Edward suspected that his father had also feared the imperious, shrewd, and quick-tempered Edward I, but not because of a drooping eyelid. He had heard the story of how his father had sought to have Ponthieu in France given to Piers Gaveston, but, fearing the King's response, he had sent a bishop to do the negotiating. The King had been outraged at his son's effrontery. Privately, learning of the episode years after it had taken place, the Prince thought his grandfather justified in his anger and his father foolish to have wished to surrender lands to a favourite.

The story went that King Edward I had been so furious that he had grabbed his son Edward by his hair and pulled out clumps of it.

"Do you want to give away lands now, you who never gained any?" the conquering king had demanded of his heir.

To lose lands was a shameful thing for a king, the prince knew; to gift them to a commoner whose loyalty offered no strategic value was sheer folly.

Prince Edward intended to gain lands, to make up for his father's failings: the defeat at the hands of the Scots at Bannockburn, and the humiliating losses of power to the barons.

What he could not make up for was his father's willingness to subvert his kingship to please two men who seemed willing to pluck the kingdom as if it were a live goose, continually laying eggs of gold for their pleasure.

"Was Grandmother afraid of him?"

The Queen Dowager had died when Edward of Windsor was six years old, and by then, she had already retired from the court to live in holy orders, devoting herself to acts of charity.

He recalled her dimly; Marguerite of France was his mother's aunt and had been a great comfort to her when she had arrived in England.

"No," Edmund replied as if the question made no sense. "She was devoted to him, although he was many years her senior. She once said that when the King died, all men died to her."

"She never married again," Edward remarked. "Nor sought a husband nor a lover. She chose holy orders instead of seeking marriage. That's odd, is it not? She was still young enough to marry and bear sons. But she abstained."

Edward remained silent. They continued to drink, both lost in thought.

25 September 1326
Hainault, Le Quesnoy Castle
4:34 PM

Philippa of Hainault walked along the rampart of her father's castle, the events of the last couple of months playing in her mind. Despite her youth, she knew that the outcome of Queen Isabella's war on her husband would have a significant impact on her own future. Only destiny would decide if the campaign would be successful and if she would one day sit on the throne of England as queen consort.

25 September 1326
Aboard a ship docked at Orwell in Suffolk
England
5:12 PM

Edward of Windsor and his uncle the Earl of Kent are still in deep conversation. Both avoiding the reality before them. That the invasion had begun.

Edmund poured wine into a jewelled flagon and placed it in front of his nephew, Edward of Windsor. He was seated at a small table that had been nailed to the floor so that, during storms, it would not move from its designated location.

"Yes," he agreed simply. Who knew what drove women to the choices they made. Perhaps his mother had had no wish to complicate the family ties that saw ambition overrule the dictates of inheritance. Edmund's mother had been fond of her stepson, and Edward II, mutually fond in return, had treated her well.

"I am to be married," Edward remarked as if this were news instead of known fact.

"Yes." The alliance would be good for English trade in the future, and as for the present, the wealth of the dowry was funding the invasion. It was not romantic, but royal marriages were not the stuff of which ballads were made.

"She is not particularly comely," Edward commented. "But she will please me, I think. The Queen arranged the betrothal."

"It will be a good match," Edmund said approvingly. "The Queen has done well. And your betrothed seems to be a sensible young woman who will be a good wife."

"She will be faithful." Edward was confident of this.

Philippa was not a beauty, but perhaps beauty was not an advantage in a wife.

She would be faithful, he believed, and steadfast. Perhaps

that was enough, as long as she was fertile and would bear him a son who could rule England after he was gone. Yes, perhaps beauty was a trait better sought in a royal mistress than a wife.

"Indeed," Edmund agreed, uncertainty evident in his voice. Edward suspected that he knew why. It was not that there was any doubt as to Philippa's virtue, for there was none.

No, Edmund was likely thinking of another queen, she who had been virtuous throughout the caprices of a marriage fraught with troubles that most royal matches did not face, until she had gone back to France, ostensibly on England's behalf. There, she had again met Baron Roger Mortimer, and the queen had dispensed of her conjugal fidelity, as if she were any wanton maidservant to be tumbled by a rogue.

Edward knew, although no one spoke of it in his presence, that the Queen his mother, was forsworn. There were those who held that she was justified in her infidelity because of the King's vice.

But the King was Edward's father; the Queen was his mother. He knew that the Plantagenets were not known for their faithfulness to their royal consorts, and he did not expect that he would change that tradition when he was on the throne. But he would be a husband to his wife, as his grandfather had been to his wives, and in return, he expected fidelity. Philippa would be faithful.

She had not reproached him for the alacrity with which the Queen had put Philippa's generous dowry to use, outfitting ships and hiring mercenaries who would accompany Isabella Capet to England so that she could mount the invasion that would place Edward of Windsor on the throne.

Edward was not sure that this was the proper use to which a dowry should be put, but he had not been asked. Perhaps Philippa did not know; the dowry came from her father, and he must have approved. There was much to be gained were the Count of Hainault and Holland to be allied through marriage with the future king of England, and Count William was no fool. He had four daughters, any of which would have been suitable for marriage. But Edward had chosen the youngest, Philippa. There were so many decisions that he was not permitted to make that this one had mattered even more.

25 September 1326
Hainault, Le Quesnoy Castle
6:49 PM

Mistress Dumont scurried across the room, fervently looking for the diamond necklace the Count of Hainault had offered his daughter, Philippa. She was in the process of doing an inventory of all the items that were to accompany them to England once the throne had been secured. Why this had to be done in advance of events concluding, she had no idea. What she did know was that she deeply resented the fact that her gentle Philippa was being thrown to an English wolf. She stopped and sighed. There was naught to be done about it; at least she had been assured that she would be allowed to travel with her charge to her new home.

25 September 1326
Suffolk, England
9:54 PM

Edward of Windsor is still musing with his Uncle Edmund over several jugs of wine. Neither of them, have yet to set foot on English soil.

"The king takes an oath," Edward said.

Edmund moved the flagon of wine so that it was closer

to Edward. Edward raised it to his lips and swallowed.

"Yes," Edmund concurred.

"First, that the Church of God and the whole Christian people shall have true peace at all times by our judgment; second, that I will forbid extortion and all kinds of wrongdoing to all orders of men; third, that I will enjoin equity and mercy in all judgments,'" Edward recited. "It's a solemn oath. It must not be broken."

Edmund was uncomfortable. He had not entered the cabin of Edward of Windsor expecting a philosophical discussion on the requirements of either marriage or kingship. One married, certainly, one did one's duty, which was to sire an heir.

Fidelity was for women; one must, after all, be sure that the sons she bore were the fruit of the father to whom she was wed.

Loyalty, whether of a noble to the king or of the king to his realm, was less ambiguous. At least, it had been less ambiguous until the barons, sniffing power like hounds on the hunt, detected the weakness of

Edward II and mounted a challenge. Fealty was not supposed to be violated. But kings were not supposed to put favourites in positions of power that threatened the stability of the realm.

Nobles, also, were supposed to remain faithful to their vows of fealty, Edmund realised with a twinge of discomfort.

He had pledged his loyalty to his half-brother in good faith. But he was not the first one to find those oaths too constricting.

The barons of another Plantagenet had forced a Plantagenet king to recognise the limits of his power.

At Runnymede, King John, the great-great-grandfather of Edward of Windsor, fuming in his fury, had signed the *Magna Carta*, acknowledging that with kingship came the responsibility of leadership. God's anointed he was in truth, but that did not justify tyranny. Those memories were ingrained in the subsequent Plantagenets, and Edward I knew the lessons his forefathers had learned.

Edward II was not the king or the man that his father had been.

It remained to be seen whether Edward of Windsor would adopt his grandfather's style of leadership or not.

There had been family discord in the Plantagenet line even back then.

Henry III, the father of Edward I, had battled a powerful baron, his brother-in-law, Simon de Montfort. But he was defeated and taken prisoner. However Edward I had escaped, and eventually, de Montfort was defeated in battle and deprived of his head.

Grandfather Edward had been young, but capable of ruthlessness when circumstances required it, but he had also been fond of his father. He had not overthrown the ineffectual King Henry III, despite external pressures. When his father died, Edward I's grief had been so great that he could not even mourn the loss of two sons, one of them the heir, who had died at the same time.

Edward I had explained his reactions by saying that a man could make more sons, but he had only one father.

A man had only one father.

The Prince rubbed his eyes and quickly drew the flagon of wine to his lips before the evidence of his weakness could be seen.

"Drink with me, uncle," he said. "A toast. Propose a toast."

Obediently, Edmund poured wine into another cup, this one not so splendid as the one from which Edward of Windsor drank. But it was splendid enough for a man who was half-brother to the king, and Edmund did not begrudge his nephew the magnificence of his drinking vessels.

Edmund hesitated. Edward of Windsor was in a very

peculiar mood, and those born to kingship were precarious in their tempers, particularly those of the Plantagenet line. Edward of Windsor already seemed more like his redoubtable grandfather, Edward I, than his feckless father, Edward II. It was unwise to venture too far from the shores of safety when in the company of kings.

"To England, Your Grace," Edmund proposed, raising his flagon. "To England, and to the puissance of those who rule her."

Edward drained his wine in a single draught.

"To England!" he toasted.

29 September 1326
Bury St. Edmunds, England
10:12 AM

The queen's arrival is a triumph, as she is greeted by English lords and members of the clergy who are reassured by her promise to restore a rightful order to the realm. Her son is the most convincing evidence of her intentions; Edward II cannot rule, but his son can assume the throne.

"Invite the lords to come and meet with us tomorrow," Isabella directed. "We must assure them of the honour of our intentions and that we have come for the sole purpose of righting the wrongs that have been done by the Despensers. We will not rest until the Despensers are removed from power."

Her messenger bowed.

"What about the King?" Mortimer asked when they were alone.

"I did not expect so large an assembly," Isabella said, as if he had not spoken.

"They say the resistance is growing. Perhaps tomorrow's representatives will be an even greater force. The more we draw to our side, the greater our chance for success. To think that even the Church views our cause as just is truly astounding."

Mortimer watched her, fascinated by her beauty. She was no longer a young woman; but her mature beauty made her all the more alluring because she was a woman of passion.

She was a queen, but when he possessed her in the hungry intimacy that made their union still so ardent, she longed to be mastered.

He had never shared his bed with such a woman. Of course, he reminded himself, he had never bedded a queen before.

What a fool Edward was, to give his paltry love to a man when Isabella offered such dazzling lust, surrendering all that she was to him, seeking only the sating of his pleasure, matching him appetite for appetite, craving for craving, as long as they were together.

Had she been this way with Edward, Mortimer wondered, or had the King's flagging affection for his wife moulded her into a woman who was a royal temptress?

Had she loved her husband in the beginning? He supposed she had; women sought love the way parched flowers sought rain. They deluded themselves into thinking that love made them whole. In truth, love merely turned them into minions, disguising the nature of their power. They failed to recognise it. But it was just as well that they were blind to their own strengths, he reasoned. Else they would rule the world.

He chuckled at the thought of the world order and how it would be turned on its head if a woman were ever allowed to match a man in rank or influence. No, it was better to keep women occupied with their rightful station in life, their bellies full with their husbands' seed, their mirrors their constant companions as they strove to retain their beauty, and thus, their husbands' fidelity.

Women failed to realise that men were not faithful by nature. Some, it was true, managed it, but most did not, unless they had a purpose.

Women were jealous and petty, and if a woman, even a queen, felt that her beloved sought another, she would never forgive him.

Edward was Isabella's enemy because he had replaced her with another; that he had chosen a man to receive his affection was an insult to his queen, and she would never forgive the slight to her sex. A woman who lost her husband to another man was a mockery.

"What about the King?" Mortimer repeated.

Rising from the bed, he strolled to the chair where Isabella sat in front of a large mirror, brushing her lustrous hair. He took the brush from her hand and began to draw it thorough her tresses in slow, deliberate waves.

"A servant should be doing this," he commented as he watched her reflection in the glass. Her eyes were closed as if he were caressing her.

"I would rather not have a servant in here with us," she replied.

Mortimer bent low and kissed her bare neck. Her maids had undressed her for bed, and in her white nightgown, she looked as innocent as a bride.

But she had dismissed the maids before he entered the room, and he could sense her desire for him. There was no purpose for such foolish circumspection, he could have told her; every royal court in Europe knew that the Queen of England had forsaken her vows and her husband and that Roger Mortimer was her lover.

"What about the King?" he asked again. "You spoke earlier of the Despensers, but you said nothing about the King."

Her lovely eyes met his gaze.

"Of course I did," she argued. "I said that we were here to restore order to the kingdom. Edward is king."

"You will need to be more specific than that, my love," he told her. Sinking to his knees, he looked up at her as if he were a supplicant. "You are so beautiful. Whatever do you find in me that lets me enter your bedchamber as if I belong there? I am not a king or even a prince. I am but a Marcher lord, a wildling like the rest of them."

The Queen bent low from her chair.

"You are my love," she returned, her voice throbbing with the intensity of her emotion. "To me, you are the king, and I your humble maidservant."

She lowered her mouth to his for the kiss that she knew awaited her. Their lips met; Mortimer rose to his knees so that he could hold her in his arms. She liked to be overpowered, he had noticed. His arms, the limbs of a man who had spent his life in the arts of war, mastering swordplay and jousting, were strong, and when he held her, she submitted to his power.

"What about the King?" he asked again, his embrace almost punishing as he held her petite body in his mighty arms. "What about the King?"

His hands knew where to touch her, the wetness between her legs already staining his fingers. She moaned with the pleasure of his sublime knowledge.

"The King doesn't matter, my love," she said. "There is only us."

He pushed his thick finger more deeply between her bush, letting her body swallow it whole. She moaned.

"But there must be a king," Mortimer murmured.

He knew that she was at the point where words were an intrusion. She didn't want to hear words. All she wanted was the vigour of his lovemaking and the consuming passion of their union.

"My Queen, there must be a king."

He withdrew his hand and she moaned in protest. Without pausing he licked his fingers clean, then fastened his lips against her, forcing her to sample her love juices.

Soon she was left breathless.

He moved back and started unlacing the ribbons of her nightgown.

"Unless," he continued as if the thought were new to him, "unless a queen rules in place of a king."

"Yes . . . " she agreed breathlessly, her love pearl throbbing from his caresses.

"But the Queen must make a public showing," Mortimer observed. "She must appear before her subjects as if there were no king."

Isabella made acquiescent sounds, but he knew she was past the ability to hear what he said.

His thick finger had restarted its exploration and now he was using it as a substitute for his hard member. The Queen moaned and threw back her head, soon she would reach the pinnacle of her pleasure.

It was better this way. He liked taking her afterwards, and imagining that she was naught but a wanton serving wench.

A wench whose sole purpose was to feel him member pump hard in her quim until he emptied himself deep within her. His shaft hardened at the thought.

He decided not to wait, but instead removed his breeches and guided his hard member to the entrance that was so willingly being offered to him. He pinch her pleasure pearl simultaneously as he entered her in one hard trust. He could feel her convulsing around him.

She would agree to whatever he suggested, as she always did, especially during bedsport, and she would be guided by him.

He started thrusting in and out, slowly at first then with all the vigour of a man who knows he is marching towards victory.

The Queen would rule. He pumped harder.

But the Queen would be ruled by him.

He held her hips still as he re-established who was the conquered and who was doing the conquering.

He started thrusting relentlessly, with the vigour of a man half his age. Her flesh yielded to his onslaught, her wetness, announced her willing surrender.

Yes, he would rule her on her royal throne just like he ruled her in her royal bed.

He did not stop to wonder, why since the start of their liaison he'd had no appetite for any other. Had he, he would have realised that Isabella was not the only prisoner of *love* and *passion* in the room.

He roared his satisfaction as he emptied himself deep inside her.

29 September, 1326
Bury St. Edmunds, England
10:58 AM

Lady Marguerite Dumont walked discreetly back to the chamber she shared with two other ladies-in-waiting in the castle quarters. She was well aware of the Queens dalliance, but it was not for her to judge. Queen Isabella had chosen her ladies-in-waiting with discernment. Each and every one of them were loyal only to her – loyal to the death.

As for her household, the punishment for confirming her infidelity or spreading the word was either death or the cutting out of the tongue. She had already proven her resolve in this matter. No one would ever dare gossip of the goings-on.

That being said, it was Marguerite's and the other ladies' duty to ensure that no one came upon the two lovers in *flagrant délit*.

29 September 1326
Bury St. Edmunds, England
7:12 PM

Prince Edward of Windsor was in another part of the castle, far from his mother's private quarters and for that he was grateful. He had barely made it through dinner. The need to put Mortimer in his place had ridden him hard,

"Shall I send for a girl, Your Grace?" the servant asked as he finished preparing Prince Edward's bed.

Edward shook his head. He was a Plantagenet and a prince, and he was no innocent.

He realised that his arrival on English shores again, with an army at his back, meant that he was regarded differently now. He was not viewed merely as a prince, as the heir of the king who would one day rule over England, as his father and forefathers had done.

He was being treated as if he were the king himself already, and a man whose desires must be assuaged, whether it was a matter of procuring a woman for the night or a kingdom for a lifetime.

"No," he replied as the servant pulled back the gold-threaded coverlet on the bed. "I would sleep alone tonight. It has been a long day."

29 September 1326
London, England
8:32 PM

The residential quarters of the Tower of London

Learning that a London mob has killed his officials and freed the prisoners, King Edward reluctantly agrees to flee west so that he can raise an army to fight his rebellious queen. He is unable to recognise the signs that he is on the way to losing his kingdom; the Despensers force him to face the fact that he is king in name only and that his life is in danger.

"She made a pilgrimage to Bury St. Edmunds!" Edward raged, pacing back and forth in front of the fireplace, his robes swirling around his long legs like miniature acolytes striving to keep up with his movements.

Bury St. Edmunds, one of the most sacred shrines in England, the abbey where King Edmund was buried after the pagan Danes had killed him, was the site of miracles performed in the name of the slain monarch. "She mocks me, and she mocks the Holy Church with her treason!"

"Have a care, Sire," said Hugh the Younger, lounging indolently upon the King's chair. They were alone, and Edward did not stand on ceremony when there were no onlookers. In fact, he did not stand on ceremony even when others were present, but Hugh did not sit on the throne in the presence of others. He was well aware of the enmity that the King's nobles had against him. He sat on the throne now with Edward's full consent.

"Your garments will get caught in the flames."

"She appeared as a widow! If she were here before me now, I would crush her in my teeth if I had no other way to destroy her! A widow! As if I were dead. I am not dead. I am the King! Hugh, she wishes me dead!"

"She is a trollop," Hugh said. "She is an adulteress and a harlot, the plaything of Roger Mortimer. She may be the daughter of a king, but she is as common as a tavern wench."

"She may be all of those things, but she has an army! I sent for two thousand men to guard the coast; less than one hundred showed up to do my bidding! My own half-brother Edmund has joined her! Henry Lancaster has joined her. Members of the clergy met her when she arrived! She spoke to them as if she had a right to do so! Do you not understand, Hugh? She seeks my crown."

"She is a woman, Edward," Hugh said in a sharp tone as

he called the king by his name, something he did only in private moments. "She cannot rule in your stead. Why should you fear?"

"She has my son with her. Do you not understand? My son is my heir. Through his veins runs Plantagenet blood. Royal blood. He will be the king when I am gone. By appearing in mourning, she shows England that she regards herself as a widowed queen without a husband."

"But you have outlawed them both! Why are you fretting over these futile shows of force? England will never bend its knee to a woman, especially a French woman, queen or not."

"Do you not understand? My son is in her power; she can do what she likes in his name. And that traitor Mortimer will rule them both! I knew his bent when I sentenced him to the Tower for his arrogance! I should have ordered his execution as soon as I had him in my grasp."

"He escaped from the Tower. One must assume that he could not have escaped from so formidable a prison as the Tower of London unless he had assistance from someone of influence," Hugh interjected.

"Yes, I know that! The Queen must have betrayed me even then. Perhaps she had taken him to her bed already. That is treason, do you hear me? It is treason! My queen is a traitor who seduces my own people with the promise of a restoration of order! What restoration can she possibly mean? I am the rightful king, and there is no one who can rule in my place as long as I am alive. And I am very much alive! Had I not already done so, I would have put another thousand pounds on Mortimer's head!"

1 October 1326
Guy's Tavern
London, England
5:48 PM

"If what you say is true, we'd best be about our business, and quickly," Jimmy Granger muttered.

"If it be true? Why, half the country has been abuzz with the news all week. Where have you been? Under a rock?" Jane Granger exclaimed. Sometimes her brother could be a proper dunce.

"You know what this means, don't you?" Jimmy asked, with a raised eyebrow.

"No, what does it mean, exactly?" his sister replied, looking at him suspiciously.

"A perfect opportunity for a revolution!" he exclaimed,

before taking a swig from his beer carafe.

"A what? Have you gone and lost your marbles?" Jane was starting to wonder why she had even started this conversation with him. It was always the same thing with that one – revolution, revolution, revolution. As if any of it would count for naught. All you ever got from a revolution was dead poor people.

"All's I know is that it has given my business quite a boost. When times are harsh, people drink even more," Jane proclaimed, putting an end to the conversation.

2 October 1326
London, England
10:12 AM

The residential quarters of the Tower of London. The King must decide to march against his unruly family.

Messengers came daily with news of the queen's invasion. It seemed to Edward as though they could not wait to bring him ever-worsening reports. Did the French woman have no sense of decorum? What sort of woman would set herself against her husband, invade his kingdom with an army, and appear in front of his subjects as if she were a widow? She was an aberration of nature; she was the vilest of her sex; she was a she-wolf, bent on the atavistic nature of an animal.

The massive doors to the king's private chambers burst open. Alarmed, Hugh sat up from the throne, then relaxed. It was merely his father.

"Your Grace," Hugh the Elder began in urgent tones. "We must flee. London has refused to rise in your support. The city has succumbed to madness."

"What are you about?" his son demanded. "Why should London behave in such a manner? Have we not sent for the city leaders to raise forces on the King's behalf?"

"I am telling you, our efforts have failed," Hugh the Elder returned. "We must flee. The mob is attacking the city. Walter Stapledon has been killed in St. Paul's Cathedral—"

"Killed?" Edward repeated, as if the word made no sense. Walter Stapledon had been one of Edward's officials, his former treasurer. Why should anyone kill him?"

"Your Grace, we must be gone, or we will face the ire of the mob, as well. They have stormed the Tower and are releasing the prisoners."

"But we are safe here," Edward disagreed. "My father fortified the Tower to withstand an assault, and my father—"

"Was not set upon by an angry mob intent upon

murder," Hugh the Elder finished. "We must escape now, while we can. We must head west, where we can raise an army in the King's name." He was speaking to his son as if the decision were theirs to make and not a matter for Edward's accord.

"I shall not leave! London is my city, and I shall stay here," Edward replied irritated.

Hugh the Elder finally turned towards his king. "London is the mob's city," he explained, as if he were speaking to a witless child. "And soon it will be Isabella's city. We must escape before that happens."

"London—what—I called upon the city to rise in my support, to come to my aid! I must have an army if I am to defeat the Queen. Are they mad; do they fail to realise that their very safety and lives depend upon me?"

"They have refused your plea, Your Grace. Men who serve you are being slaughtered by an unleashed mob that cannot be brought to reason. If you stay here, you will be killed."

Edward stared at the Despenser. "They cannot kill me. I am the king. Anyone who sheds royal blood will be punished in my courts and by the Church, as well."

"Listen to me, Your Grace. If your blood is shed, much solace it will be to your unquiet shade to know that your murderer is being punished. And do not be so certain that the killer would suffer. Members of the Holy Church have joined the Queen. We must go west if we are to have any hope of surviving. Hugh, see that we have sufficient means to make our way. We shall need to buy allegiances. Your Grace, I suggest that you waste no time if you want to live to fight the Queen for your throne."

In bewilderment, Edward turned to Hugh the Younger, who had already gotten down from the throne and was making his way to the doors. "Hugh, why are you leaving?"

"Because I've no wish to end up like King Edmund the Martyr," Hugh replied. "There will be no miracles issuing from my dead body."

"You are not a king," Edward explained. "No miracles would come from you."

Hugh paused at the door. "Edward," he said, with ill-disguised impatience. "You must face facts as they are. We are hated in London, and you are despised. Now London can show us what it thinks of us, and the end to that is a coffin. I have no wish to die so that a hideous mob of madmen may vent their anger on my person."

Edward followed Hugh out of the room.

"You are asking me to leave the capital city of my kingdom because of an unruly mob? Do you think me so

69

craven?"

"I don't care if you are or are not, Edward. I've told you; we can stay and die, or we can escape and fight. I choose the latter. You must choose for yourself."

Edward stared at the man he loved, disbelief evident in his gaze. "You would leave me?"

Hugh sighed. "Not willingly," he answered. "But I will not stay and meekly be slaughtered. We will go west, where we can marshal support for our cause. We will find soldiers and fighting men who have not been seduced by the madness of this unholy quest of the queen to take your throne." Setting his hand on his monarch's arm, Hugh the Younger continued his cajoling. "Is it not true that plans were laid for Your Grace to make his way towards the March of Wales to rouse the good and loyal men of that land towards his cause and to punish the traitors? We need to do just that."

Edward gave Hugh an appraising look, then nodded. "We shall go to Gloucester," he finally conceded. "And I shall write to the Pope. He will not tolerate this unwomanly behaviour. He will chastise Isabella for her forwardness."

"Write quickly when there's time," was the response as Hugh led the way out of the long, dark hallway. "But there's no time now; a letter from a dead man will persuade no one."

9 October 1326
Suffolk Countryside
England
10:08 AM

"Did you hear the latest?" Benjamin Rand asked the foot soldier who was standing next to him, polishing his equipment.

"The latest about what?" the man replied, looking bewildered.

"Them royals have gone and lost their minds. Now Queen Isabella's put out her own reward. Two thousand pounds on the head of Hugh Despenser the Younger."

The other man just shook his head in disbelief. "Let's hope this insanity doesn't include hours of marching across marshlands. My equipment is already heavy as it is, and this blasted English weather is not only making my bones creak, but also ruining my leather!"

13 October 1326
Oxfordshire, England
9:19 PM

Isabella is infused with the rush of success as she marches to Oxford. Mortimer senses the power that is within reach. But for Prince Edward, who realises that in order for him to be king, his father must be removed from the throne, the jubilation is hollow.

Queen Isabella was more demonstrative in her affections than she had ever been before in the presence of her servants and her son. She caressed the bearded chin of Roger Mortimer, letting her fingers linger over his lips.

"More wine!" she called. The colour in her cheeks was high, as if she had already had more than enough to drink. But the euphoria she exhibited would have shown itself even if she had drunk nothing more than water. Her son couldn't understand what emotions were driving this strange and manic joy, but he didn't like it.

The servant brought another bottle and filled their goblets, but when he approached the Prince, Edward shook his head. He had had enough to drink. There were no longer any limitations on him; he was nearly a man now, and if he wanted to get drunk, his mother would not protest. But he did not want to be drunk. He was not entirely sure that he wanted to be sober, either, however.

The queen dipped her little finger into the goblet and removed it. Raising it to Mortimer's mouth, she inserted her fingertip between his lips. Mortimer, his eyes hot with desire, licked greedily as her finger went deeper into his mouth.

"Your head is worth one thousand pounds, my Lord," she said, her French accent more noticeable today than usual. "I wonder what price the King has put on each delightful feature. Your eyes . . . your ears . . . your nose . . . " As she listed each one, she dipped her finger once more into the goblet of wine, caressed him with that finger, and then leaned close enough for their breaths to intermingle without them touching. "I baptise you," she laughed, kissing her fingers and then pressing them against his lips.

Prince Edward made a sound of disgust. Hearing him, the queen remembered suddenly that she was not alone. She drew back in her chair, pulling away from her lover.

"You must understand, *mon fils*," she began in a tone of pleading persuasiveness, "that the dear baron was my only hope when I escaped to France. Had I not left, I don't know what my fate would have been. The Despensers were determined to take everything I had; they had already taken the lands that were mine, that had been given to me by my Aunt Marguerite. If we are to right the wrong that has been done by the Despensers, surely you can see that we cannot be hesitant."

Perhaps he would have more wine, after all. Prince Edward signalled to the servant, who drew near upon his command. The servants were obedient, Prince Edward noted. As they should be.

He'd noticed that his father's servants seemed to wait to make sure that whatever King Edward told them to do met with the approval of the Despensers. His father hadn't noticed, but Edward had, just as he'd noticed the sly, knowing smiles of the servants at his uncle's court when they saw the Queen and Baron Mortimer together. It angered Prince Edward to see servants so bold that they dared to allow their thoughts to show. Prince Edward knew what they thought. They thought his father a weakling; they thought his mother a strumpet.

But when he was the king, he would rule as his grandfather had ruled. No one had sneered in his grandfather's presence; the great Edward I was fair and generous to his servants, but never did he behave in a manner that failed to meet the expectations of kingship.

"I shall offer a prize of two thousand pounds for the head of Hugh Despenser!" His mother's voice, louder than usual (due to the influence of the wine, Edward suspected) rang out in the hall.

Mortimer roared with laughter. "Which one?" he jested. "The son or the father?"

"The son," the Queen said, and all at once, there was no mirth in her tone. "I shall see him executed. I shall watch as he is castrated, and I shall watch as his intestines are removed whilst he is still alive. I shall not even blink for fear of missing a single moment of his pain. I want to hear every cry and groan that comes from his lips. I shall watch as they draw and quarter him, and I shall—"

"Surely you will not," Prince Edward objected.

"I will," she insisted stubbornly.

"But you are a woman. Such sights are not for a woman."

"I am a woman who has suffered much at his hands," she whispered, looking neither at Edward nor at Mortimer, but at the flickering flames of the candles on the table.

They had eaten their fill, and the servants had cleared the platters away. The cooks in the kitchen were skilled at their craft; Mortimer had patted his stomach in pleasure after he had eaten. Prince Edward's appetite was lacking; he ate a little, but what was left on his plate would give the dogs a hearty meal.

"I shall watch him die with the greatest pleasure, and it will still not atone for what I have endured."

"The question is moot, Your Grace; you have already put a price on Hugh the Younger's head, remember." Mortimer's cajoling voice rang clear. "Unless you would like to put another one?"

Isabella clenched her fists, then took a deep breath and shook her head no.

"What of the father?" Mortimer asked, taking a cluster of grapes from an ornate silver bowl that the servant had placed on the table. "Surely you want to see him die, as well. Despenser the Elder is as much your foe as the Younger."

"Yes, but I do not need to watch," Queen Isabella said carelessly, accepting a grape from Mortimer's hands.

"The father did not steal my husband from me."

"Any man who would allow himself to be stolen from the likes of you is a fool," Mortimer replied softly. He took another grape and held it poised in front of the Queen's lips.

"With the Despensers gone, we shall rule England as it should be ruled," Queen Isabella said, turning her head to smile at her son. "There is much to change, but I am confident that you will do it."

He wanted to smile back at her. She was his mother. But

what of his father, now in flight from London? A son he owed his duty to his parent; as a prince, he owed fealty to his father. And yet, here he was, at the table with the man who sought his father's downfall. Was he motivated by love for the queen, or the desire for the power that he envisioned?

Prince Edward thought of Philippa, loyal, docile, and kind. She would never have cause to turn against her husband this way. He would not be a perfect husband, the prince knew. But he would be a husband.

"With guidance, of course," Mortimer added smoothly. "The Prince is young, and youth must be instructed properly. It will be good to be in power. Enough of this supplication at the courts of others. We shall not have to go a-begging."

Isabella looked at him. "No, we shall not!" she agreed fervently. "To be a queen who begs is yet another affront caused by the Despensers that is unpardonable. God himself will bless me for what I have suffered. To have my mail read by that sneaky spy, Eleanor de Clare; to have my children placed under the authority of the Despensers; to have myself, a queen, the daughter and sister of kings, subjugated by those fiends . . . " She stared into the flames of the candles again, as if there were something within the fire that only she could see.

"God will forgive me," she said.

Mortimer's knowing eyes met Prince Edward's. "You have nothing to be forgiven for," he assured her.

"Your husband failed you as a man. He failed England as a king. You have the courage to restore what has been lost. Boadicea herself was not more courageous than you. She rose against the Romans to defend her people and to avenge the abuse she and her daughters had suffered at their hands."

Queen Isabella was not familiar with the legends of the English. She merely smiled at her lover's flattery.

Prince Edward rose from the table.

"According to my tutors, Boadicea died," he said curtly. "I do not wish to see my mother suffer the same fate."

13 October 1326
Near Bristol, England
10:49 AM

The queen and her growing army are in Oxford; the king and the Despensers have fled Gloucester and are on their way west to raise an army, but their hopes and their options are dimming. King Edward finds himself peculiarly nostalgic, beset by memories of the past, when he was the one making the choices. He chose Piers Gaveston and Hugh over Isabella because he preferred their love to that of any other, and now he struggles to validate his choices. The queen should have been more obedient to her husband's will; it was not her place to overrule him. The fault is hers, for her disobedience. To see matters otherwise would be to accept his failings, the failings that severed his relationship with his father.

He was a king in flight. It was all very well to say that he was raising an army to fight the invasion of the French-born queen and her Marcher lord lover, but the word was spreading that the English were flocking to Queen Isabella's side. She and Mortimer had reached Oxford, and that was entirely too close to Gloucester. So Edward II and the Despensers were once again on their way west.

79

He still had supporters; he was not entirely abandoned. Lord Powell, a half-Welsh, half-English noble whose castle was near Bristol, had welcomed Edward warmly, offered him the sanctuary of his castle, and after ensuring that the King and the Despensers were fed and their needs seen to, had bid them good night.

"I was born at Caernarvon Castle. My father was fortifying the defences against the Welsh, and my mother was not a woman to allow the rigors of childbearing to intrude upon her duties as queen. Where the king went, she went. They say that my father promised the Welsh a prince who did not speak a word of English," Edward reminisced. "I was three days old when he brought me out to the Welsh leaders and presented them with their prince." He chuckled at the memory. He had heard the story so often that he no longer knew if it was true, or merely one of the many legends that had sprung up around Edward I. But it was a story that he enjoyed.

Hugh Despenser the Younger had heard the tale before. Too many times, if the truth be told, and he had no patience for worn-out stories of a dead king. He held out his goblet. "More ale," he said to the king. "It's an inferior brew, but I've raised a mighty thirst since we left Bristol."

King Edward, still mulling over the story of his

presentation to the Welsh, obligingly poured more ale for Hugh, oblivious to the fact that a king did not serve his subordinates.

"We shall go to Bristol," Hugh the Elder stated confidently. "We shall raise a force, and we shall have the west behind us."

"We shall have to go somewhere," Hugh the Younger concurred sourly. "We can't stay here, and we can't return to London. That she-wolf has seduced the country. We never should have consented to let her go to France, and we were mad to let the Prince go."

Despite his use of the pronoun, it was clear that Hugh the Younger did not regard the fault as his own. When the Queen's letter had arrived, requesting that the Prince be sent to France to do homage for his father's French lands, Hugh had been willing, just as he had been eager to see the Queen leave England. Edward would not bring that up now, but he remembered.

"We had her in our power," Hugh went on, aggravation plain in his voice. "We knew when she wrote letters to her brother. She did not have the revenues from her lands because we were vigilant in denying her money that she would have misused. She could not turn the royal children against their father because they were in our care. We had everything we needed to maintain order in the realm. We were mad to lose control of the Queen. It was like a chess game, and any chess master knows to watch the queen, else she triumphs. All that has transpired since she went to France has happened because we did not keep her under our command. Women must be ruled."

An image of the Princess Isabella as she had been on her wedding day came, unbidden, into King Edward's mind. Young as she was, she had been a girl of blinding beauty. Even Piers, when he had met her after the bridal couple returned to England from France, conceded her beauty. She had been blessed not only with extraordinary beauty, but with wisdom, as well. She had mediated when Edward's troublesome barons overstepped their bounds, and she had done so, he knew, for his own benefit.

She had given him four children. She had been a good queen during those years. He wondered if, perhaps, matters would have been less corrosive between them had she been less jealous of his friendships. Should she not have occupied herself with a woman's duties and not sought to meddle in what she could not possibly understand?

Privately, Edward did not understand it himself. He could not explain why first Piers Gaveston, and then, after Piers was gone, Hugh Despenser the Younger, summoned the ardour and affection and loyalty that his wife did not. He clenched his fists as he thought these unkind thoughts. He loved Isabella, but she could never have been enough. If only she hadn't come upon him and Hugh sharing pleasures right after he had left her in bed, unsatisfied. Nothing was ever the same after that.

Edward shook his head.

No. HE was KING. The fault was hers.

Had he been blessed with a woman as virtuous and supportive as his mother had been, surely he would have followed the path of his father, the brave king and warrior, the adored husband. Surely he would have done so.

"Women must be ruled," Hugh said again.

Edward, lost in his reverie, simply nodded.

"I agree. But I cannot rule a woman who is leading an army against me."

"She is not leading the army," Hugh asserted. "She is merely a pawn. Mortimer is a man and a soldier, and it is he who brings the enemy against us."

"They have my son," Edward replied. Nothing could ease that pain; whether he resorted to anger or admitted to his hurt, he could not assuage this sorrow as readily as he excused choosing Hugh Despenser over his wife.

"Prince Edward is old enough to know where his duty

and his loyalty lie. He is your son and your subject."

Edward closed his eyes.

What would his father have said of this catastrophe? To have a son and a wife leading an army against their liege, lord, father, and husband was a blight of unknown measure. So many times in his youth, he had disappointed his father.

On his deathbed, Edward I had made his son promise that he would be strong against the Scots. But Bannockburn had seen the end of that. Edward II silently resolved that he would forgive his own son. When his armies were triumphant and the queen and Mortimer disposed of—he would give Hugh leave to take care of that as he chose—he would welcome the Prince back as that Biblical father had welcomed back his prodigal son. They would talk, and Prince Edward would be given the opportunity to acknowledge his guilt and his contrition.

As king, Edward would be magnanimous and forgiving. His father had not been so with him, yet Edward II, for all that he was not Edward I, would be a better father.

But first, he had to defeat his son and the forces of is wayward queen.

13 October 1326

Lord Powell's residential quarters (Bristol), England
10:54 PM

Lord Powell looked to his wife, who was already tucked away under the sheets, and sighed. She had been locked up in their bedroom all day, feigning illness.

If truth be told, she wanted nothing to do with the king and was counting the hours until he and his entourage were on their way.

"Are you asleep, my lady-wife?" he whispered as he began to undress.

"How do you expect me to be asleep in this infernal racket?" his wife retorted sourly.

"You are quite right, darling, but as you well know, they will be gone tomorrow."

"Hmph," his wife snorted. "I hope you took an inventory of what they ate and drank, so His Grace can reimburse you once he is back in London."

"There was no need, my love. King Edward had with him a chest full of coins. If I were a betting man, I would estimate that it was nothing short of thirty-thousand pounds." Lord Powell finally had his wife's full attention. She looked at him, wide-eyed.

"And this you tell me only now!" she shrieked.

Lord Powell winced. "Yes, dear, I found out a mere moment ago. But rest assured, any outstanding debt will be settled by the monarch on the morrow."

His wife pursed her lips. But by now, Lord Powell had had enough. He was quite done talking about the king. The only reason he overindulged his wife was for these secret moments, when it was just the two of them, and she submitted willingly to his naked desire and will.

"Come here," he whispered hoarsely. "I need tending to." His wife frowned and looked away, but they both knew it was all pretend; she needed his possession as much as he needed to possess her.

15 October 1326
Wallingford, England
09:32 AM

Continuing her inexorable march to the throne of England, Queen Isabella stops at Wallingford. Her army has grown, the king is in flight, and she no longer needs to hide her purpose. She envisions herself as the regent, ruling England as she mentors her son in the role of the future King of England.

"My people!"

The queen's voice rang out over the crowd that had assembled upon her arrival. The nucleus of mercenaries and foreign troops that had made up her army when she had arrived in England had swelled to include English nobles and soldiers who saw in her the hope of the nation. The first Edward had inspired his people with his achievements, but the second Edward had none of his father's virtues. Nor did he partake of the vices that one would expect of a king. The bond between King Edward II and the younger Despenser puzzled the ordinary Englishmen and troubled the nobles. Wenching, gambling, and drinking were all common sins that the titled lords shared and excused in one another.

Their confessors knew better than to expect their masters to seek forgiveness for the sins of manhood. But for the king, the sovereign symbol of England's might, to behave as a woman in the company of the despicable Despenser, was a violation of his royal blood. Prince Edward, tall and handsome, might be a mere youth, but he showed promise of following his grandfather's character and not his father's ways. His mother, the daughter and sister of kings, was merely a woman, but she was undoubtedly royal and would look out for her son. That was what women did.

"Men of England!"

The crowd quieted. The Queen was dressed in her royal finery. She was a beautiful woman, worth looking at. She stood on a platform in front of the people. At her side was her son.

"The trials of England cannot continue! Our nation has been plundered by the avarice of the Despensers, father and son. They have made themselves rich at the expense of the nation's bounty. They have despoiled the treasury, squandered our military prowess, and trampled upon the rights of our people. They must be brought to justice!"

The crowd cheered at this. They were not enamoured of the barons, who were arrogant and lawless, but when did anyone ever expect charity from the likes of the wellborn? Yet nobles and ordinary folk could meet on common ground when the subject was the Despensers, who were known for their greed.

"The Despensers have done far more than that," the queen continued. "They have violated God's order, as well. Not only have they come between the king and his people, but they have come between the king and the vows he made to God when he made me his queen. Marriage is a bond between husband and wife, and as long as the Despensers divide us, I must protect my son's rights, even if that means denouncing my duty as a wife. I must be a queen and a mother before I am a wife!"

The nobles who had flocked to the queen's banner were listening closely. They rather liked the prospect of having a youth on the throne and his mother at his side. Edward I was not a monarch who could be ruled by his lords, but the boy and the woman would be easily managed. The nobles all had wives and sons, but they ruled their households, and they saw the prospect of rule over the crown, as well. As for Mortimer . . . They knew well enough what he was about. His ambition was not hidden. He influenced the queen, to be sure, but women were easy prey to their foolish notions of love. Doubtless, Mortimer was planning to become the power behind the throne, but the barons could have told him that the space behind that alluring structure was apt to be crowded.

"The Despensers must pay for their sins! They must not be allowed to circumvent my son's rights as the heir. He is the rightful ascender to the throne. He will not be swayed by the vile profligacy of the Despensers; he will rule as his grandfather ruled. He will be mighty in battle, just in his rulings, generous in rewarding those who are loyal to him. I have watched my son grow into young manhood, and I have guided him as a mother who values the rites of kingship. I am a king's daughter. I am a king's wife. I will be a king's mother!"

The men of the assembly, and the women, as well, who had gathered to see what weighty matters were taking place in the centre of their town, roared at this promise from their beautiful queen. She would restore the crown to order. She was a mother, and those who remembered Queen Eleanor, the stalwart, fertile, and beloved wife of the first Edward, were nostalgic at the memory Queen Isabella conjured.

"People of Wallingford! You have witnessed the story of England from this castle. As far back as the Saxons, Wallingford has been a bulwark of the nation. Wallingford Castle has watched as royal battles have waged, but Wallingford Castle has never fallen!"

The citizens of Wallingford cheered at this praise of their town. The battles between King Stephen and the Empress Matilda were long past, but it was through the line of Matilda and her husband that the Plantagenet line had come to power.

"Think back upon your history, people of Wallingford. You remember when Wallingford Castle was gifted to Piers Gaveston. When Gaveston was executed, King Edward gave the castle to me." The queen nodded as the crowd clapped, whistled, and shouted, uplifted by the importance of their castle in this current struggle for justice. The comparison between the detested Gaveston and the rightful queen was well-placed; the citizens of Wallingford could take pride in their queen's ownership.

"Wallingford shall be our mainstay," Queen Isabella vowed. "From this castle and this town, we will set forth our just cause and trust to God's providence for our success. My son will rule England with all the honour of his heritage, and he will make England proud of their heritage!"

She held out her arm to gesture at her son, who, at fourteen years old, was already taller than his mother. Edward's youth was no obstacle to his poise; kingship was in his very veins, and he stood before the throngs, composed and regal, as the people showed their support. The crowd was wildly enthusiastic. The queen had made her purpose known, and the English were satisfied. She had been wronged by the Despensers; she, of royal birth, had been shamed and debased by the father and son who had deluded her husband in a manner that was unfathomable. But it was through the queen's maternal guardianship of her son that England would be made right again, and the third Edward would follow the ways of the first Edward.

Reassured that all was well with England, few in the crowd noticed Roger Mortimer, almost hidden in the crowd.

But the barons took note of him.

15 October 1326
Wallingford, England
11:32 AM

Eleanor de Clare 1st Baroness le Despenser, was running. Never had she thought she would have to surrender the Tower of London to an unruly mob, but this was about to become her reality.

Suddenly, she stopped in her tracks. She was the granddaughter of a king and the beloved niece of a king. She could not just run and hide.

She should have expected this end. Uncle Edward had taken her husband, Hugh the Younger, and now they were gallivanting about the countryside trying not to enter into a direct confrontation with Aunt Isabella. Eleanor knew the truth of it. She was Uncle Edward's favourite, after all. He paid all her expenses when she was at court, and even sometimes when she wasn't. That privilege had increased once he began to share her husband. Eleanor bit her lower lip.

The arrangement had taken some getting used to, but

after all, she well knew that she shared her husband with not only the king, but with various wenches, as well.

Having married at the tender age of thirteen, she herself had known no other lover. Despite the numerous children she had borne him, Hugh's insatiable appetites were not something she could quench.

Yet he still found time to regularly and diligently ensure that she had no need for a court lover, and that was all she demanded.

At the noise of the angry mob, she snapped back to reality. What would they do to her? London had been rife with untrue rumours of an unnatural relationship between her and her uncle; would the mob take out their anger upon her? No, she would seek protection from the prisoners. As she realised the brilliance of her idea, she smiled.

Currently, the late Bartholomew Badlesmere's nephew, Sir Bartholemew Burghersh, was locked up in the Tower. His brother was Henry, Bishop of Lincoln, and he was currently with Aunt Isabella. If she liberated Bartholomew, surely he would protect her from the queen's wrath.

15 October 1326
On a ship from Chepstow

England
11:32 AM

The King and Hugh Despenser, still seeking a base and an army, have crossed the border into Wales and are on board a ship, on their way to Lundy. They realise, but will not voice, the fact that England is denied them and they must seek support in Ireland.

"This foul weather will see us shipwrecked before we reach Lundy," Hugh complained as the ship rocked upon the rowdy waves. He was in the king's cabin; the ship's captain had insisted that King Edward go below because it was too perilous on deck. But Edward had been reluctant to leave. He was no coward, he'd told the captain. But the captain had pressed his point; the men were better able to fight the storm if they were not worrying over the safety of the sacred person of the king. Conceding the wisdom of this, Edward had agreed to return to his cabin.

The cabin was small and confining. Edward felt as if the walls constrained his height. The movement of the ship and the noise of the storm made it difficult for him and Hugh to hear one another when they spoke, but Edward's head was so filled with the recent events that his favourite was unable to command his full attention.

"She has made my son *Guardian of the Realm*," Edward said, his voice almost breaking at the thought of his son usurping his kingdom. "She has pushed me aside as if I matter for naught."

"When we raise an army in Ireland, she and the prince will both be made to remember that they live but for the pleasure of the king. The time for mercy is past, Edward. They must be punished for their boldness."

"Guardian of the Realm." Edward repeated his own words. "London, my city, my capital, is hers."

"London was hers the day the mob stormed the Tower," Hugh said impatiently.

"No, not formally. Yes, there was a mob, but they were not unified. Now they have declared for the queen. They have turned against us."

Edward was seated on the bed. It was fortunate that he would not have to sleep in it, because his long, lanky form would have dwarfed the mattress.

"I have lost the city," Edward mourned. "How can a king be restored if he has lost London?"

"Listen to me," Hugh ordered, grabbing the king by his brocade doublet. "We will be restored to power. You will not lose heart! You are the king and the son of a warrior. Would you see a woman and a boy best you?" He shook the king angrily, but Edward, although his head and shoulders moved jerkily in response, was lost in the painful reality of what was to come.

"You are the king!" Hugh bellowed as the ship tossed on the waves and the noise of angry nature clamoured outside. "You sound like a frail woman!"

"No . . . please, Hugh," Edward moaned, covering his face with his hands. "Do not speak such harsh words to me. Please, I implore you! Everyone has turned against me. I cannot bear it if you also abandon me."

Hugh Despenser released the king's doublet and stood back. The gale outside was so powerful that it pitched the ship forward into the waves. Hugh lost his balance and fell upon the bed, on top of King Edward, who was curled up in a foetal position.

"Listen to you," Hugh said disdainfully. "Is this a king who will rally supporters? Will you weep and sob when you beg soldiers to follow you?"

"No, I will not," Edward finally whispered, wiping his streaming eyes with the sleeves of his robe. "I will be as much a king as ever my father was. You will be proud of me. The soldiers will see my father in me, and they will rally to our side."

"That's better," Hugh approved. "My father will hold Bristol for us when we return with our forces. We will use Bristol as our base, and from there, we will regain all that the she-wolf has taken. You must not be meek. You must be firm and punish both mother and son. If you are weak, he will be ruined. I shall tend to his punishment; you are too likely to submit to your tender feelings."

"Yes, Hugh, whatever must be done. We shall reclaim the throne together, and once we return to London, we shall no longer have to deal with an unnatural queen."

Restored, Edward rose from his crouched position.

"You have dared speak to your king as if addressing a commoner, Sir Hugh. For that, there must be consequences…I expect your submission." Leisurely, he let his eyes linger on his favourite.

Hugh knew what this meant. He had seen this yearning look before. If truth be told, he did enjoy a lot of their trysts. Bedding Edward gave him a heady rush of power. However, lately, it had become a nuisance.

That said, as he had done countless of times, he would submit to his liege's carnal needs, but even in the act, they both knew that Edward was the one who was conquered.

"Do remove your breeches. I believe that this time, I will

mount you without the ointment or sweet words," Edward whispered, his underpants already filling up.

The gale was so loud that they did not realise anyone was pounding upon the cabin door until the winds died down and they could hear the noise.

"Enter!" Edward called out, irritated that the chastising of his favourite would have to be postponed.

It was the ship's captain. "Your Grace," he said, bowing as he entered. "The storm is too fierce. I fear for your life. We must return to land."

"Return to land? But I must raise an army, and I cannot do that unless I go to Ireland," Edward objected in dismay.

"Your Grace, if it were safe to travel, I would venture forth without fear. But the winds are against us, and it's folly to continue. You cannot raise an army from the bottom of the sea."

"Can you not continue?" Edward questioned the captain. "I must gather my army."

"Your Grace," the captain pressed, reluctant to gainsay a king, "I am no craven. I have sailed in many a storm, and I have lost men to the waters. We are ordinary men; if we die, the fortunes of the nation do not change. But if aught should happen to you, we are at fault. Kings must be protected, Your Grace. We may be commoners, but we know our duty before God."

Edward clenched his fists. "Very well; bring us back to land. You are brave to speak up to a king, captain. I will not forget your courage."

The captain bowed and left the cabin.

"I fear, Hugh," Edward remarked. "I fear that the Fates are against us."

"It's a storm, Your Grace." Hugh opted for formally addressing the king. With any luck, that would soften the coming punishment somewhat. "It is not a divine pronouncement. Storms rise upon the waters, but only fools look for portents in them. We shall return to land, and then, when the storm subsides, we will once again sail to Lundy, and from there to Ireland."

Edward nodded. His thoughts were his own. Would it have been so bad if he had fallen overboard in a raging storm and met his death? Would anyone have cared? Would it not have been better to meet his death with Hugh at his side?

This was not a notion that he could share with Hugh, but in the recesses of his heart, Edward wondered if death sometimes came not at once, but in stages, so that by the time the final stage arrived, a man welcomed it.

He shook his head, to clear his thoughts. He was not yet ready for death.

Taking a deep breath, he focused on his favourite. He had not missed Hugh's reverence, but it would not save his rear-end from a proper seeing-to.

Edward had recently discovered that mounting Hugh mercilessly and frequently did wonders for the anxiety and stress generated by his rebellious family.

He reached out his hand and pulled Hugh's breeches so forcefully that they ripped apart. With no additional words spoken, he bent him down towards the bed until he was on all fours. His smooth bottom was a magnificent sight to behold.

Any thoughts of the coming calamity fled the king's mind. Whilst he punished Hugh ruthlessly with his member for the next half-hour, all he could think about was the promised ecstasy that always followed after filling the younger Despenser to the brim with his seed.

15 October 1326
Wallingford, England
11:32 AM

Prince Edward's youth is swiftly vanishing as the battle for royal power wages between his mother and father. The king falls as the queen rises, but for a boy of fourteen, the son and heir, loyalties blend and divide. Family ties present a confusing web of loyalties; Henry, the earl of Leicester and soon to assume the earldom of Lancaster which his brother formerly held, is the cousin of King Edward and the uncle of Queen Isabella. For Prince Edward, trust is fragile, and he strives to discern the nature of loyalty in a time of conflict.

"Your Grace, shall I accompany you?"

Prince Edward shook his head as his horse was brought to him. Wallingford was bustling with the activity engendered by the looming rebellion, and everywhere he looked, he could see the livery and pennons of his mother's supporters. For the Prince, the bright colours and heraldic insignias were as familiar to him as the men they identified.

They were the lords of England, the titled men whose families and lands were part of his own history. Many of them were relatives of the King, such as his kinsman Henry, a grandson of his great-grandfather, Henry III, who had offered to join the prince on his ride.

Henry, earl of Leicester, was a man in his forties. He was

used to influence and power, but he had been loyal to Edward II when his older brother Thomas, the earl of Lancaster, had rebelled. After the execution of Thomas as a traitor, Henry had petitioned for his brother's lands. The King had given him the earldom of Leicester, and he had seemed satisfied.

But now he had abandoned his cousin, Edward II, in favour of the Queen. Royal retaliation had come swiftly, as the Edward II in response had sent Hugh Despenser the Younger's son to seize Leicester's lands.

The grounds at Wallingford were fairly littered with the growing number of such men, who saw in the queen's invasion a chance to stop the power of the Despensers. They were not, they had assured Edward of Windsor earnestly, against the King. They joined the Queen to bring down the favourite. They tolerated Mortimer only because there was no other option. He was the queen's ally and her military representative, and it was more political to leave matters at that level.

"Your Grace," Leicester said, taking hold of the horse's reins. Prince Edward was unsure as to whether his cousin intended to help him mount or prevent him from doing so. It was symbolic of the ambiguity of loyalty, which shifted according to the winds of the moment. "The Queen does not think it safe for you to ride alone."

"The Queen has named me *Guardian of the Realm*," Prince Edward objected. "If I am such, why should I need a nursemaid to ride with me? I can sit in a saddle, my lord."

"I meant no slur against your horsemanship, Your Grace," Leicester said. "I refer to the sacredness of your person. You are the heir; you cannot take risks."

Prince Edward took the reins from the Earl's hands. "Not take risks? I remind you, cousin, of what we are doing. We are rebelling against the King," Prince Edward stated with deliberation.

"The King left the country, Your Grace," Leicester returned. "The Queen named you *Guardian of the Realm* because the land must not be without a king. He left."

Edward had heard the argument. Incessantly, the his mother and Mortimer had preached and cajoled, persuading him that the departure of King Edward from England had required the Queen to install him in his father's place. It was easier to acquiesce to their logic than to allow himself to be plagued by the torment of doubt.

Prince Edward expelled his breath in a long, ragged sigh. "He returned to Wales."

"A storm drove him back," Leicester answered. "I beg you, allow me to accompany you." Leicester took advantage of Prince Edward's pause to call for his squire to bring his horse.

Prince Edward recognised that he was obliged to succumb to the Earl's intention. As he waited for the horse to be brought, he looked over the grounds. The atmosphere was infused with a sense of waiting eagerness; the men, their swords and lances, their battle readiness, were all part of a whole.

This was an army, preparing to go to battle in the name of England, under the aegis of the Prince. How could they all be so certain? They had sworn fealty to the king; the allegiance that the lords owed to their king was sacred. Yet they were here, ebullient with purpose, as if loyalty oaths were something that could be transferred facilely simply because the king had a son to whom they could swear their oaths.

Leicester mounted his horse with the ease of a man inured to the saddle. Prince Edward led the way out of the camp; as he passed, the men raised a cheer. The Prince nodded in acknowledgment of their voices, feeling as he did so that he was playacting. He was not the king. He was the heir.

As they left the grounds, the land opened up into fields being harvested. Peasants, stolid and loyal to the soil they tilled before they gave obeisance to the men who sat on thrones, did not look up from their labour as the pounding of horses' hooves thundered upon the ground. His father was often been mocked for his strange affinity for the lower classes.

He was a Plantagenet, not a peasant, and to share the pastimes of the commons was a form of abasement. Prince Edward understood this. There was much that he did not understand, but he was of his class, and the peasants existed to serve and to build the kingdom.

Prince Edward and Leicester galloped at a lively pace for a time, until they reached the crest of a hill, and the earl brought his horse to a halt.

"Prince Edward," Leicester said.

"I pray you, cousin," the Prince replied, holding up his hand in warning, "lecture me not. If I am *the Guardian of the Realm*, I am not subject to the lectures of my elders."

"I would not presume to lecture my liege lord," Leicester replied.

Prince Edward merely answered him with a dismissive gaze.

Leicester had the grace to smile ruefully. "Very well," he conceded. "Perhaps lecturing is inevitable in a man of my age. You cannot think it was easy to turn to the Queen instead the King. Both have claims of kinship, but now I decide as an Englishman."

"I am told that you are styling yourself as Lancaster now, the title of your late brother."

Edward heard all the news of the lords; Mortimer recited the details to his mother daily, the information part of his litany in a worship service designed to demonstrate to his mother how thoroughly just her cause was and how the lords of England sought to avenge their grievances by joining her.

Leicester did not reply immediately. He appeared to be lost in thought, gazing down in apparent fascination at the tableau of humble workers reaping the fruitfulness of the lands in the fields below.

"The title was my brother's and should be mine," he said finally. "King Edward knows this to be so. To have Despenser take it from me is an insult."

"Is not disloyalty more than an insult?" Prince Edward countered.

"You are a youth, Your Grace, and — "

"My lord," Prince Edward interjected formally, "a youth took your lands. Do not be dismissive of those who lack years."

"I meant no disrespect, Your Grace. I serve you."

The Prince wondered if he would ever regard a declaration of service with other than a sceptical eye. "Do you serve me for a restoration of your Lancaster title?"

"I serve you because you are the heir to the throne of England. I will not serve a false king. But you are born to the crown, Your Grace. The queen has declared it so."

"Yes."

"The queen has been a loyal consort to your father. She has supported him in times of great urgency and travail. Few women could summon forth such courage."

"She has the support of Roger Mortimer to strengthen her resolve," Prince Edward returned. He was deliberately circumspect in his words. Perhaps he meant exactly what he had said, and there was nothing more in his words than recognition of Mortimer's experience and skill. Or perhaps his words were a challenge poised upon the edge of a verbal spear.

If the latter, Leicester was apparently able to tilt the spear aside. "When you are on the throne, Your Grace," Leicester said firmly, "you will have loyal supporters who will be honoured to offer advice when you seek it. It does not demean even a king to accept counsel from men he trusts, whose experience and leadership are known to him. I offer you my advice if you ask for it, Your Grace. But my devotion is offered to you always. England needs a strong king, such as we had in your grandfather, Edward. A strong king makes the nation powerful; a weak king diminishes the land."

"You deem it a choice?"

"God rewards strength, Your Grace."

This was inarguable. God was somewhere in all of this. The bonds of father and son were inviolate, except when the duty of a king intervened. What was Edward first? A prince, a son, or a servant of God?

"When you are king," Leicester added, as if it were an afterthought, "you will not require the tutoring of Mortimer."

17 October 1326
Cardiff, Wales
11:48 AM

Aware that his kingship is ebbing away, King Edward II is beset by an aggrieved sense of betrayal. His family has deserted him. His error came out of his clemency; he should have disposed of his enemies before they had the chance to rise against him or poison his family.

It seemed as if his kingdom had shrunk to this single castle where he and his faithful servants, the Despensers, were lodged. His family, his capital city, his lands and possessions were all aligned against him. That a king of royal lineage, in whose veins flowed the revered blood of Edward I of the Plantagenet line, of the saintly Edward the Confessor, of the valiant Richard the Lion-Heart, should be thus reduced was a betrayal of the sanctity of the monarchy.

"I should have executed him," Edward muttered.

"You ought to have executed the lot of them," Hugh the Younger concurred. "We would not be in this state had the traitors been punished before they joined your faithless wife."

"They were not traitors ere this!" Edward pointed out in exasperation. This was not a new topic. Hugh had been bemoaning the fact that the traitors had been alive to go to the Queen in the first place, but how could Edward have known what they would do? He had thought them loyal. And although he would not voice the thought, he wondered whether more of his lords would have stood by him had the Despensers been less avaricious in their yearning for lands and wealth.

It seemed that, although he was king, he did not have enough goods to sweeten his nobles' craving for luxury, demesnes, and prestige. How did one keep a ravenous horde of wolves sated? he wondered. How had his ancestors done it? What would his son do when it was his turn to keep the wild pack at bay, attentive to his command but wary of his rage should they fail him?

King John Lackland had known the defeat of his power at the hands of his lords. Edward took some comfort in knowing that, although he was abandoned and without succour, his barons were not meeting him to force him to sign a document that would cede his power. John had truly been hated.

Of course, he had not had to address the faithlessness of his queen. But John's father Henry II had.

Queen Eleanor, duchess of Aquitaine, of renowned beauty, lands, and accomplishments, had been just as unwomanly in her duty, siding with her sons against her husband and leading rebellions against Henry II. Legend said that the fair queen had been less than observant in her conjugal vows. But Henry had killed a priest, a dark stain upon the Plantagenets.

Were they still paying for that dreadful sin? Edward wondered. Henry had done penance, and surely the sin was expiated. Did darkness haunt the Plantagenets, and was he the latest member upon whom the light had been doused?

"The mob beheaded Stapledon with a breadknife," Hugh told Edward, his voice harsh with the venom of hatred and rage. "They brought his head to the Queen."

Edward knew this. His spies kept him aware of all that was happening in London and in the Queen's entourage.

"She hated Stapledon," he said absently.

"She gave his head to the goddess Diana!" Hugh was furious. "Yet the church flocks to her side."

Edward doubted that Isabella had done any such thing. Where in Gloucester would she have found a shrine to a pagan goddess? Stories grew like wild weeds around royalty; one could not believe all of them.

"You should have done to all of them what you did to Lancaster," Hugh continued.

The earl of Lancaster. Thomas, the king's cousin.

Yes, Edward had been decisive and bold then. And yet merciful, when all was said and done. He had not, because his cousin had royal blood, subjected him to the drawing and quartering that his crimes deserved.

But he had been deliberate in his planning, although that was nothing to bring up to Hugh.

Thomas, one of the Lords Ordainers so intent upon separating Edward and Piers, and so determined to reduce the power of the throne to nothing so that their own insolent arrogance could thrive, had had Piers taken to Blacklow Hill; there he had been run through with a sword and beheaded. His death had been ignominious and shabby.

111

Had Thomas of Lancaster noticed that his death mirrored the execution? Edward had ordered a chaplet placed upon his head, a mocking parody of a crown, and had had him placed upon a run-down mule. Facing Scotland, a fitting dishonour for a traitor, Lancaster had surrendered his head. It had taken more than one swing of the axe to do it, but that had only made the punishment more fitting, the vengeance for the sake of Piers all the more memorable, even if no one but Edward perceived it.

And now, Henry, brother to the disloyal Thomas, had followed suit and turned against the king.

"I intend to," was Edward's long-awaited reply.

"If ever we can leave Wales," Hugh interjected.

"You have lands here," Edward reminded him. "I should think Wales is where you would seek to be."

He had thought Wales would be rife with Despenser loyalists who would rally to the crown, but he did not say this. Hugh had been oddly truculent on the subject of his Welsh holdings and people, and it was apparent that this was not where he wished to be.

"Wales is not England, and Cardiff is not London." Walking away from his king, he said over his shoulder, "The Queen has sent for your young son John of Eltham."

"I heard," Edward answered wearily. Did Hugh think

him deaf? They had both been present when the spy had returned with the account of what had gone on in London. Now both their sons would be under Isabella's control.

"Eleanor could not hold the Tower."

"How could a woman hold the Tower against a mob?" Hugh asked with a raised eyebrow. "She was at risk."

That cut.

When they left London, they had not expected the city to fall into such chaos. London was the bedrock of English heritage. It had withstood all manner of violations, invasions, and ills. And Edward certainly would not have left Eleanor de Clare, of all women, to such danger had he been aware of what was going to happen.

Eleanor was his dearest, most beloved, favourite niece. Had he not given her, his most treasured niece, as a wife to his dear and best friend?

She was Hugh's wife, but Hugh had not thought of her safety when fleeing the Tower and leaving her there with the king's ten-year-old son, John.

Edward was glad that Isabella had sent for their son, he was safer with her, than with a crazy London mob. He did not, nor did Hugh, mention that Eleanor had been imprisoned in the Tower. She was not allowed to leave, the spy had told them, lest she be pregnant with the King's child.

Edward had protested volubly against such a pernicious rumour. Hugh had been strangely silent. The spy had been paid and sent on his way, and the matter was not brought up again. Edward's thoughts turned back to the matter at hand. Lancaster, the Bishop of Hereford, and so many others were marching with the queen, on their way to Bristol.

But Hugh the Elder would hold Bristol. He was ruthless and shrewd, and he would not be defeated. Isabella would know that she was beaten when she failed to take the city, and that would be the turning point that Edward was waiting for.

18 October 1326
Wallingford, England
10:44 AM

The queen, her son, and her lover are heading for Bristol, where they know that Hugh Despenser the Elder is defending the castle. They are confident of victory, but this will be the first time that the queen will encounter one of her hated enemies, and she must make her case to her supporters. She instinctively knows that what will work here is what worked at Bury St. Edmunds, where, dressed in mourning for her lost marriage, she successfully established the guilt of Despenser the Elder. Roger Mortimer agrees, and her lover's approval is all that Isabella needs.

"Perhaps my son should address the troops," Isabella suggested.

She and Mortimer were finally alone in the queen's bedroom. The day had been spent meeting with the English lords who had come to her side, vowing that she had risen against her husband the king because he had failed her as a husband, and then broadening her charge to detail how he had failed the land as its monarch. She was left to protect her son's inheritance against the Despensers.

Then she had met with the clergy, assuring them that she had sought nothing so much as to be an obedient and faithful wife. She had reminded them of the episodes when she had mediated the quarrels between her husband and the English nobles. She had travelled with him and on his behalf, risking her life; she had nearly been captured by the Scots. When returning from a pilgrimage to Canterbury and in need of a place to rest for the night, she had been denied entrance to Leeds Castle by the king's enemies. Isabella's history was well known, but now the men who had left her husband were hearing for themselves what she had endured as a faithful consort.

Mortimer shook his head. "That would be unwise," he told her.

"But why? Surely the lords will be more likely to reckon the justice of our cause if they know that they are serving the true heir."

"They already know that, my love. Has young Edward not been at your side as you have presented yourself to the people? But it is unwise to remind battle-tested nobles that they go to war against a king who, however flawed his judgment, is nonetheless a man, and not a boy. If you allow the boy to speak as their king, they will see for themselves that he is callow and green."

"My son will rule wisely," Isabella argued. "Although he is but a boy, he will grow into manhood."

"Where he will be guided by us," Mortimer reminded her. "He will benefit from our knowledge so that, when he is old enough to serve without a regent's supervision, he will know what to do and how to avoid the mistakes of his father. He has far to go, however, before he can match his mother in wisdom. You were brilliant, my beloved queen, in having the prince brought to France to do homage for his father's lands."

He rose from the bed and went to her side. "No seasoned counsellor could have made such a shrewd decision. You are as wise as Deborah, my dear one. Who better to guide a prince on his way to becoming a king? But if you let the boy address the troops, who among the nobles will recognise the sagacity of a mother? They will seek power amongst themselves, and their quest will be for their own gain, not for England's weal. They do not have a mother's love; would you subject your son to their machinations? He must govern, but he must not fall prey to their rule. You would not wish for the prince to become, like his father, the victim of a favourite like the Despensers or Gaveston, who will rule the realm from the royal bed."

Isabella clenched her fists. "Do not!" she begged. "Do not speak of it!"

"We must, my love," Mortimer returned. He curled his hands around the circumference of her head, miming a coronation. "You are my queen," he told her in a low, husky voice that presaged the state of his desire. "The queen of my heart, and of my homeland. I will be ruled by you, and by the son born of your body. But you, knowing the weakness that comes from the king, must be vigilant against its manifestation."

"There is no indication, Roger—you have not seen any

signs, have you? Roger, you must tell me!" Isabella clung to her lover, finding, as she did, solace in his physical strength.

"No, no," he soothed, as his fingers ran through her tresses. "Nothing. But he is yet young, and he must be guided by his mother. Would you cede your authority to that of the English nobles, who are apt to have motives that are less than pure?"

"Hold me," she whispered, looking at him beseechingly. "When you hold me, I can forget all that has happened and all that Edward has done.

"You've been a gracious queen and a forgiving wife," Mortimer murmured.

"Piers Gaveston was not vile like the Despensers," she replied, knowing to what he referred. "But after he was gone, we were content together for a while. Piers Gaveston never sought to deprive me of my rights as the queen."

"Gaveston was not the fiend that Despenser is," Mortimer agreed. "I have cause to be grateful to Gaveston, for when my father died, I was placed under Gaveston's guardianship by King Edward I. But I can recognise the difference between Gaveston and the Despensers. Can your son? They have been with his father for much of his life, and he is but a boy."

"Edward heeds my counsel," Isabella insisted.

"Of course he does." Holding her in his arms, Roger Mortimer was a fortress protecting her from the calumny outside their intimacy. "Of course he does. But do not delude yourself, beloved; to the lords of England, you are but a woman, and you have already performed your duty by giving birth to the heir. They will not regard you as an equal in the game of thrones."

Mortimer continued to embrace her with one arm, while the fingers of his other hand stroked her lovely hair, combing through the abundant locks to bring the tresses tumbling to her shoulders. "But you with me is yet another matter altogether. Together, we will guide your son wisely."

Assuaging the queen's fears whilst conjuring her passion was an unfailingly successful means of managing her emotions. Mortimer was adept at plying her body with his touch, as he reminded her of how great her need was for him.

Surrender was bliss. Isabella allowed him to lead her to the bed and undress her in the sweet fury of desire. Her anxiety faded, replaced by the hunger for his touch and the power of his body ruling over her. He was correct in his assessment, of course; she was a foolish woman to have thought that Edward, her son, should be put forth as the leader of this war. He was a boy with much to learn from a seasoned warrior like Mortimer, a man who would protect

119

her son from the selfish motives of the nobles, who would line their pockets with plunder if they could manipulate a boy king.

Mortimer trailed his hand over the queen's pink nipples; she moaned like a tavern wench. With little preamble, he snaked his hand down and inserted a finger into her hairless quim. She was already juicing copiously. He would mount her hard today, just the way she liked it.

Even as he pumped his hard member at a relentless pace in and out of her, his thoughts were elsewhere. When she cried out with her release, Mortimer smiled but did not desist. He liked the thought that, after her pleasure, she was now naught but a woman forced to service his needs. In fact, he made sure this was always how their trysts ended, by covering his member in a special ointment that kept him hard for longer. The queen moaned at his continued use of her. Mortimer ignored her.

It would be as he planned. The queen would rule her son, and Mortimer would rule the queen. For he, better than any man alive, knew how much she feared the flaw in Edward that had allowed the Despensers to suborn him. He knew her fear; he knew her need. She loved her son and wanted him to be a good king. Her motives were pure. But she was a woman, and women were subject to men; the Bible said so, and who could dispute the word of God? Mortimer was now panting. The thought of how sore the queen would be from his misuse made his member even stiffer. He pumped harder.

Adam had fallen because he listened to his wife; therefore, men were designated as the lords of the earth. Mortimer would fulfil his destiny, a destiny that would make him, through the queen and her son, the ruler of England. That final thought pushed him over the edge, and he emptied his bollocks deep inside the Queen of England, ensuring she received every drop of his seed.

20 October 1326
Bristol, England
2:32 PM

The siege of Bristol has begun. The queen and her forces, now grown from a small invasion force to a representation of the most notable families in England, have assembled outside Bristol. Inside the city is Hugh Despenser the Elder. Isabella, mother and queen, must deliver herself to the lords as a woman capable of resolute action. She must

convince them that she is not a weak and powerless female;
she is the future regent.

What were they thinking inside the castle? Isabella wondered. What was it like to be powerless after years of overweening might and to look out upon an assembled army, knowing that the Queen of England was the leader?

Did Hugh Despenser the Elder tremble at the thought that the woman he had despised and abused was now in the ascendancy? The king could not shield him; the king wasn't even with him.

"We wait him out," her uncle, Henry of Lancaster, said in response to her unspoken thoughts. "He cannot stay inside forever. We will wait. You will be free of your tormentor soon, Your Grace. His tyranny will soon be over."

The Queen nodded. The city of Bristol would not surrender without a fight; Despenser would not be cowed. She could not speak for fear that her emotions, which could not be forestalled by the unfeeling prudence that men displayed, would overwhelm her. Mortimer had warned her that she could not succumb to her tender side.

"You are a mother, and the queen," he had said, "but you must be staunch in your goal. Despenser is your target, and nothing can sway you."

She had wept under the strain, but Mortimer had stayed firm. If she would rule, she would only convince the lords that she could do so by doing away with her tender emotions.

When she appeared in front of her army, she kept Mortimer's words in the back of her mind.

"He has wronged our person greatly," she said. "As he has wronged us all," she added, mindful of the need to remind her supporters that they were all victims of Despenser's greed and ruthlessness.

The earl of Norfolk, who had chosen the queen over his half-brother the king, looked on in grim silence. Hard choices were for strong men to make, and he had made his, but there were always consequences to decisions that involved royalty.

Yet even the mightiest king could be petulant; the nobles could not be toyed with. It remained to be seen how this grandson of Edward Longshanks would suit the throne. In the meantime, the nobles would not be sitting idly by. But first, the nation had to be rid of the contagion that the Despensers had infected upon it.

"England's very air will be purer when the Despensers are no longer breathing it," muttered the Earl.

The barons and lords had long memories. It was not, after

all, so long ago that they had forced the Despensers into exile. After the execution of Piers Gaveston, the nobles believed that they had effectively conquered the problem of royal favourites.

But the Despensers coveted power in a way that Gaveston had not. They wanted power and wealth, and the King had been willing - nay, eager - to give them both, at the expense of the lords themselves, who lost estates and money so that the Despensers could be supplied.

The Marcher lords, a law unto themselves, opposed the rise of the Despensers; it was then that Roger Mortimer had rebelled against the King with the intention of bringing down the Despensers.

"Had we prevailed in 1321," Thomas of Brotherton, the earl of Norfolk said to no-one in particular, "we would not be here today." It did not sit well with him, this *coupe d'état* against his half-brother. But he knew well its necessity.

Rapacious and insatiable, the Despensers had wanted more. After taking land from England's nobility, they had then won the Queen's lands, as the King willingly deprived her of her possessions and revenues, all to please the Despensers.

Barons were executed, women were imprisoned and deprived of their lands, others were charged with debts of sums so enormous that payment was impossible. In the end, five months after they were sent away, the Despensers came back from exile more powerful than they had gone away.

"Whatever we need to do to win, we shall do," Norfolk concluded, his voice ringing of resolve.

Isabella, fortified by the knowledge that she and Mortimer had already concluded this, nodded.

The announcement, false but effective, that the queen and her army travelled with cardinals and a papal bull granting absolution to those who fought against the king, with excommunication being the fate of any who opposed the queen's army, was convincing.

It carried a whiff of logic, as Prince Edward, the undisputed heir, was with them. The undecided viewed the presence of the heir as confirmation of the ecclesiastical authorisation; to fight to put the rightful king on the throne was to serve God.

"With the Despensers gone, England will be rid of its tyrants." Roger Mortimer strode to the front of the group.

He did not reference the King; he referred to the Despensers. The vagueness of his speech, coupled with his unexpected but not unintentional positioning at the Queen's side, conveyed multiple messages to the lords.

"Where is the Prince?" Henry of Lancaster asked

pointedly. "Should he not be here?"

"He is here," Queen Isabella assured him. "There is no need for him to be with us now, however."

Mortimer had schooled her well.

The prince should not be present among the council as they carried out the martial plans, or he would think himself experienced, when he was but a novice.

He should not be in the company of the leading nobles because they would find a way to manipulate him. He must remain under the authority of his mother.

He was, after all, a boy, not a man, and this war was a man's business. Besides, Mortimer had said, what if he were regarded as a rebellious son, violating the commandment to honour his father? Such a transgression could be held against him by the church.

"This is kingship," growled Norfolk. "He needs to learn. His boyhood is about to come to an end."

"Of course," the Queen said brightly. "He is the heir."

"He'll be among us the next time we meet," Lancaster stated firmly. He didn't ask the Queen to confirm this, and he deliberately ignored Mortimer, who was not a man to take kindly to being ignored.

The atmosphere fairly crackled with the tension of men seeking to mark their own spots in the proceedings. What petty things men were, Isabella thought, and was shocked by her own perception. They could never endure womanhood and the travail that accompanied the members of the opposite sex.

She was a queen, born to her royal status and yet treated as if she were no more than a maidservant or a brood mare. However, she was the mother of the boy who would become king, and the lords of England would learn that her son was not to be played with by puppet masters.

"Bloody siege," complained Sir William Trussell. "We could be in the grave before it ends."

"No," Mortimer said confidently. "Bristol will fall. There is no hope for Despenser. The city will fall, and he will be in our hands."

"And he will die," the Queen added. Her face was set in such an expression of firmness that she could have been posing for a portrait. As the English lords looked upon her, they saw that only punishment by death would satisfy King Edward's wife. Despenser the Elder would be the first to face her virulent enmity, but no one present could deny that the right was hers.

"Yes, Your Grace," Lancaster agreed. "He will die, and his son, as well."

No one mentioned the king. But every man present was

thinking of him and wondering what fate would befall a superfluous king.

Isabella alone was not thinking of Edward. For herself, she asked no mercy. She was a faithless wife and a stalwart mother; she would pray to the Blessed Virgin that her actions should bear joyous fruits for her son.

25 October 1326
Bristol, England
11:22 AM

The city is about to fall, and when it does, Hugh Despenser the Elder will meet his fate at the hands of a vengeful queen and the nobles of England, who are eager to make him pay for his actions. But the nobles of England realise that they must not rid themselves of one favourite for another, and they meet in secret to discuss the dangers of the ambitious Mortimer and his influence upon the queen.

The army would sleep well that night. It was obvious that the city could not hold out any longer. Hugh Despenser would not be able to stave off the queen's army. Henry, now confidently taking the title of *Earl of Lancaster*, that was his due and that, he was sure, the queen would grant him, walked through the camp. The men were inside their tents, the banners of their liege lords outside as a signal of their allegiance.

Lancaster, the hood of his cloak pulled low over his forehead, passed through the gathering without being noticed. An army camp had an atmosphere that could be read as if it were script, and Lancaster knew that the men were anticipating victory upon the morrow.

They were the fortunate ones, he thought as he walked swiftly to his destination. They fought, lived or died, bandaged their wounds or celebrated their triumphs, and went on their way to the next war or home to their fields.

Not for them was the next stage that would follow; after the battlefield came the council chambers. This was a different form of battle, one fought not with blood but with one's wits. The past was ever present, as the heroes of one generation became the traitors of the next. It was nimbleness that was required. As long as a man managed to keep his head attached to his neck, Lancaster thought, he would thrive.

He saw movement ahead in the grove of trees on the edge

of the city. They were early. Nonetheless, even though he knew the men who waited, he kept his hand on the hilt of his sword. Caution was always necessary.

His dark cloak blended easily into the trees. The others, like himself concealed by their dark clothing and the trunks of the clustered trees, were familiar to him. He was related by marriage or ancestry to any number of them; their heritage was an incestuous mélange of titles, babies, and graveyards. Their unity made them of one mind.

"Mortimer," said Norfolk.

"Yes."

"He means to rule."

"Of course he does. A besotted queen in his bed, a boy king dependent upon him for guidance. . . Who would not, in his place, expect to wield the reins of royal power?"

"We do not rid ourselves of Despenser merely to leave an opening for the next favourite."

"No, we do not. But we must proceed judiciously. Edward II still reigns. Despenser the Elder remains in Bristol. Despenser the Younger is with the King. Prince Edward is a youth. It will do no good to be rash. First Despenser the Elder. Then Despenser the Younger. Then the King."

"But not the same fate, surely?"

Lancaster frowned. Some things were better left unsaid. One did not speak of the murders of anointed kings. Whether or not that was to be Edwards fate was yet to be decided.

"There are some matters that Mortimer will, no doubt, attend to," he replied. "Perhaps it will be in our own interest to wait and see."

"Allow Mortimer to have all that power? Have you lost your wits?"

"Mortimer can be of service to us for a time. He may attend to matters that, ultimately, will be his undoing. Mortimer fancies himself the power behind the throne."

"The power between the queen's legs, more like," one of the men said, sniggering.

"There has been too much power lost and claimed in royal beds," Lancaster declared with impatience. "Are we servants, to tangle ourselves in bed sheets? I think not. We have the opportunity to serve a king, the grandson of Edward of esteemed memory. But in order to set Edward of Winsor upon a clear path, someone else will need to clear away the refuse. Why should we soil our hands, when Mortimer is likely to be more than willing to do it for us?"

"What are you saying?"

"I'm merely saying that we must be patient. If Mortimer

131

sees his way to power for a time, we must bide ours. The Prince will not be docile for long; nor will he be a minor forever. The chronology may be a trifle out of sequence, and we will have a king who is not yet deemed ready to rule, but what of that? The queen and Mortimer will dispose of their enemies as fate allows, and none of us need sully our hands. When Edward sits on the throne as his own man, we will be, in truth, his faithful lords and servants."

Lancaster allowed the import of his words to sink in. Although all of the men gathered in the woods were known to one another, no one referred to anyone else by name. It was wiser to remain anonymous in such an enterprise.

"Are we followers or leaders?" asked a man.

It was a fair question.

The English barons had suffered at the hands of feckless kings who ruled by whim rather than wisdom, but it would have been false to claim that the lords were above reproach. Powerful men who controlled their own lands were ill-suited to meekly follow the edicts of injudicious kings, and for every strong, shrewd Edward I, there had been a John. The problem lay in the fact that a lord of his land was both follower and leader, owing fealty to the king and demanding it of his own knights. That blurred the lines, Lancaster supposed. But he was not a philosopher, and it was not for him to define the hierarchy by which England was governed.

"Both," he answered without hesitation. "We follow the king. If he leads us well, we follow. If he does not, we must lead, else all England falls." He knew that it was a flawed response, but nonetheless a diplomatic one that recognised allegiance and explained rebellion. So it was to be an Englishman.

"We're not de Montfort," he went on, swiftly cutting off that line of thinking, lest any of the men covet a role that would doom them. "We have a king to follow."

"Which one?"

Lancaster cursed silently. Too many questions, too much thinking. Why could they not see that the easiest path was the patient one? The Queen had invaded the realm, and by doing so, had conjured a rebellion against the King. The king's subjects, weary of the Despenser greed and illegal acquisition of power and possessions, had flocked to her banner. She travelled with her lover, an overly ambitious, proud Marcher lord, and her son, the legitimate heir.

The Queen was competent enough, Lancaster acknowledged, but she was a woman, and England, which had rejected Matilda generations before, would not accept a woman on the throne. Nor, though the lady likely did not realise it, would her lover, who plainly had aspirations

133

beyond the queen's bed.

But the only obstacle to the Prince's rise was his age, and that would be remedied with every day he lived, provided that he was given proper instruction. To Lancaster, the road was plainly marked. Let the Queen reveal the weakness of her sex; let Mortimer overreach himself; let the Prince mature. In the end, the Queen's inexperience and Mortimer's arrogance would solve the messier problem of the King's continued existence, and when the Prince came into his own, he would be ready, and his nobles would support him.

"Wisely and cautiously, my lords," Lancaster advised. "Return to your men and wait for the morrow. The downfall of the Despensers begins."

"The Queen will be given credit for it," grumbled one lord, averse to a woman taking precedence in matters that were better suited for men to master.

"Let her. The lady has been greatly wronged by the Despenser father and son. Why should she not claim her victory over them?" Lancaster asked magnanimously. "Would any of you who have daughters begrudge your own her revenge against such a monster? They must be destroyed."

"And the King?"

Stupid fool, Lancaster thought. Why speak of what everyone inwardly knew? There was safety in silence.

"We mean no harm to the Lord's anointed monarch," Lancaster said piously. "We seek the safety and good wealth of England. Our forefathers demand no less than our loyalty."

It was a good answer. It said nothing, but it did so magnificently.

27 October 1326
Bristol, England
10:15 AM

With no hope of rescue and no chance of escape, the city has surrendered, and Hugh Despenser the Elder is in the hands of the queen's forces.

There would be no clemency. The verdict was known in advance, and no one would stand in the way of the queen's determination to punish Despenser.

There was no interlude between the acceptance of the

city's surrender and the arrest of Hugh Despenser the Elder. Still wearing his armour, he was brought into the room where his trial would take place.

Isabella watched as her enemy was led to face his accusers. His helmet was taken off to reveal the features of a man, no longer haughty and brutal, but old. That surprised the Queen; she had not thought of him as old. He had only been her tormentor, ageless as sin.

She smiled. Despenser met her eyes and then looked away, for her triumph was so apparent that every man in the room recognised it.

She did not trouble herself to conceal her pride; this was no time to be demure. All the humiliations that she had suffered in the past might have been invisible to others, but to Isabella of France, the daughter, sister, and wife of kings, the offenses mounted a tower between the two of them, and as she looked at him, she saw his violations. And he knew what she saw and knew that the die was cast.

"Hugh Despenser," intoned Sir William Trussell, "Earl of Winchester, you are on trial. You are forbidden to speak just as Thomas, earl of Lancaster was when he sat before you to be judged. Your transgressions against the Crown and its subjects have brought you to this point."

Despenser, encased in his armour, looked tired and pale,

almost frail, as if, were it not for the metal he wore, he would have had nothing to support him. Isabella had wanted to see him punished immediately, and the nobles had agreed. What point was there in waiting? He was going to die, of that there was no doubt and the sooner the better.

No one needed to say that Despenser the Elder was not the only quarry they would be hunting. He was but the first one to be captured.

One by one, his accusers named his crimes. It was a long list, and nothing was omitted.

They were sentencing a man to death, and justified though they knew his death to be, the judgment could not be flawed. The law was the arbiter of his fate, not the lords; they were merely the vessels by which the judgment would be delivered and carried out.

The lords of England were ruthless by nature and pious by creed, a peculiarly effective mix of characteristics for the dispensing of legal justice.

Queen Isabella, watching and listening, did not care if they were fair or not. She knew his guilt. There had been a time when she and her husband had truly been as one. Edward's flaws and his favourites had not been the mechanism that had sought to rob her of her place as Queen of England. The Despensers had done that, and while the father was not the vile fiend that his son had proven to be, he was an enemy nonetheless.

"In her mercy, the queen has ruled that pardons will be issued . . . " Sir Trussell paused. Despenser's face revealed a glimmer of interest, as the suspense of the sentence and the inevitable hope that life would go on exposed his apprehension. "...to all those who were falsely accused by you of crimes that they did not commit. But you, Hugh Despenser, Earl of Winchester, are sentenced to death. To be hanged."

Hanged.

To die, in full view of his accusers. Isabella nodded. But not merely hanged.

He must know his punishment so that there was time, while he still had his head and the wits within it, to dread his fate. His fear was as vital to her as the ultimate end, for she had known such fear for so long that it seemed there was not enough time for him to experience what she had endured. Therefore, the sentence must be that much worse so that, as he was taken to the place of execution, he would suffer the anticipation of horror, knowing that every step brought him closer to pain beyond bearing and humiliation past tolerance.

"To be cut into pieces," Sir Trussell spoke solemnly in

the silent room as each man absorbed the sentence that had already been agreed upon, "and fed to the dogs."

Eagerly, the queen watched Despenser's face, and then she saw it - the first flicker of mindless apprehension as he considered what this meant. The human body, whole and complete, was easily understood. But who could comprehend the concept of his own dismemberment, his body cut into sections, limbs and torso dripping blood onto the ground beneath? At what point did the senses feel the pain of the noose? What would it be like to face the hangman, knowing that when life was gone, one's body would be severed, one's blood would flow from the gaping hole where flesh had only moments before contained the force of life? When, as the noose tightened, did the mind cease to think? As life ebbed, would his final thoughts be of what was to come? Would he imagine the grotesque destruction of his body? Would he regret what he had done? Would he plead with God for forgiveness?

Their eyes met again. The queen did not know how she looked to him, but she knew that at last, he feared her. Hugh Despenser had met his fate in the form of a woman, and Isabella of France was his judge.

The lords had no qualms about watching as the noose was fitted around Despenser's neck. They were men of battle, hardened to death. They had inflicted it with their swords and spears, and they were familiar with the body's capitulation in the grip of mortality. Still in his armour, Despenser's body fell out of life and into the vast, open absence. His body surrendered its fluids, and the smell of his excrement filled the cool October air.

The lifeless body was laid flat. Where once there had been a man, there were now sections of flesh, the ragged seams of skin split by the unerring slicing of the executioner's sword.

There was blood, so much blood that even warriors blanched. But Isabella did not. She watched without a tremor as the man who had transgressed against her royalty and interceded in her marriage was expertly separated from his earthly body and his life.

The head, removed from the broken body, was raised by the executioner and held up to the crowd. The tyrant was dead. Isabella's gaze was unflinching as the head was positioned on a spear.

"The head of the tyrant will be taken to Winchester for public display, to warn of the fate that befalls those who sin against the laws of the land," Sir William Trussell said and thus concluded the execution.

It was a wise gesture to make, but it was also one that Isabella made from her own heart. The Despensers had treated England like a Christmas goose, to be plucked and stabbed and devoured for their own satisfaction, and many people had lost more than they could afford to do without, merely so that the father and son could profit.

How could Edward, who was not in his heart an unkind man, have been so cruel? How could he have turned his back on his duty and given into his own desires at the expense of others? The queen felt as if the man she had married and the man he had become could not be the same.

"My love," Mortimer murmured when they were alone again that night, their private celebration of the victory they had achieved lasting long hours. The wine had flowed freely, and it was not a night for abstemiousness. "We are invited to Hereford, to stay with the bishop. I have heard that my cousin Arundel is there."

"Does it matter?" Isabella asked, distracted from her thoughts. "We must put our minds to capturing the remaining Despenser."

"Arundel has been a supporter of the King; he must be punished."

"Many lords have supported Edward, but that does not mean all are traitors."

Mortimer's hands on her shoulders were firm, a grip that seemed almost oppressive. "Arundel is a traitor, I know it, and he will pay."

"My beloved, we cannot do away with everyone who has not joined us. When we are in control of the kingdom and my son is crowned, then we will expect allegiance."

His fingers dug into her shoulders. "We must expect it now. Arundel must acknowledge us."

"Will he not accept my son as king?"

Mortimer didn't answer. For a moment, she wondered if Mortimer at times forgot that there would soon be a third Edward on the throne, and that Edward's son would be king. Of course, he would need guidance, and who better to guide him than Roger Mortimer?

Mortimer would protect her son, she told herself.

14 November 1326
Caerphilly Castle, Wales
11:32 AM

The victorious forces of Queen Isabella are relentlessly claiming England for Prince Edward. The king and Despenser the Younger are inside the castle, but Edward is anxious, and Hugh feels that they must flee, even though it means leaving his eighteen-year-old son Huchon in charge of the castle to face the forces of the queen.

"Monsters! They are monsters!" Edward raged.

The news of Despenser the Elder's death had travelled quickly as far as Wales. Hugh's grief at his father's death was tinged with apprehension. If that she-wolf was so bereft of womanly tenderness that she could watch without emotion as a man was dismembered, beheaded, and fed to the dogs, what would she do to the man who had stolen her husband's affections?

"They will stop at nothing until they have done the same to us," Hugh Despenser the Younger warned. "We must get away from here."

"And go where?" Edward queried.

"Farther west, of course. We can escape them. We must escape them. Do you realise what she will do to me if I am captured? You are at least the king, father of the heir."

"As if kings have never been killed for the sake of expedience," Edward replied absentmindedly. "How can we leave? We are settled here; our possessions and wealth are here. We cannot take everything with us, and we cannot do without funds."

"I'd rather have my head," Hugh retorted.

Edward laughed without humour. "Truly? I find that hard to credit. I have never known you to seek a Spartan life over one of luxury, and yet now you are willing to do without?"

"Huchon will hold the castle," Hugh said confidently. "This is not Bristol. He will hold the castle for us until we can return in triumph."

Triumph. What would that be? How could the king regain what he had lost?

"Huchon!" Hugh summoned his son, who came at his father's call. "I am leaving you in command of the castle. It's true that the queen is likely to send her curs here seeking the king, but we shall be gone long before she arrives. Caerphilly is a fortress; it will not fall. You must not surrender."

"Father, what if she is after my head and all of those who reside here?"

"You are a boy. She is a woman," Hugh scoffed. "She will not harm you. But you can see that I must go. Her quest for vengeance is ravenous. We will leave our possessions here, and you must guard them."

"Father—"

"Mind that no one takes a penny or a jewel," Hugh cautioned. "The money—the queen must not lay her hands upon it."

There were twenty-seven barrels of money in the castle holding fourteen thousand pounds. If the queen got hold of that, she'd be in funds for her ambitions. Edward had heard from his spies and messengers that she was already plundering the estates of his supporters, who were now being treated as if they were traitors. Traitors against the anointed king. The audacity of the woman!

"I should have thrown her overboard when we left France," he said hotly.

"Your Grace?" Huchon asked.

No answer was forthcoming.

"We must leave. But you must guard what we leave behind and keep it away from the Queen," Hugh reiterated to his son.

Huchon wondered exactly how he was supposed to do that, but his father was a whirlwind of activity as he went through the castle, ordering the servants to gather up certain belongings and to pack others away. Edward, seeming lost in thought, followed in Hugh's wake, apparently content to allow Hugh to determine what they would bring with them and what they would leave behind.

"That foul Jezebel plundered my stores like a cursed Viking raider," Hugh swore. "She took two dozen of my golden cups from the Tower. My belongings! She has no

145

right to those things. She can pilfer someone else's goods."

"She's done the same to Arundel's possessions," Edward commented. "And money, as well."

"Father—" Huchon called, but Hugh, having made his way through his chamber, was already gone. Huchon looked doubtfully at what was left behind: a red robe with bears embroidered on the fabric, a black cap adorned with pearl butterflies. What the queen, if she stormed the castle, would do with such garments, he could not guess, but as he had been charged with keeping her from doing so, he ordered the bewildered servants to pack the items away.

"We leave, now!" Hugh announced. The horses were saddled, the goods they were taking with them packed, and the servants—pitifully few now—waiting for the signal to depart. Edward took some comfort in knowing that he had paid his servants the night before. Some of the servants would stay on at the castle, but others were accompanying him. He was still the King of England, and he travelled with an entourage of valets, a sergeant-at-arms, and clerks. He would not be shamed.

Once again, they were heading farther west, intent upon putting miles between them and the queen. The king was not without adherents, and there were supporters along the way who were willing to provide him with their hospitality.

He was grateful to them for their kindness; Hugh, however, railed against them for the treason of those who had abandoned the king.

"Sir," replied his host that evening, "these are not our crimes. We have remained faithful to His Grace, and we shall continue to remain so."

"You say that now," jeered Hugh, his face flushed from anger and the excess of wine that he had taken with his meal.

"But when the she-wolf comes with her pack, you will all be as meek as sheep. We are served by curs and by cowards."

"You, sir, are not served at all," the man replied sharply. "We serve, as do you, the king."

Hugh stared at him. "You would not have dared speak to me thus a month ago," he shouted.

"A month ago, my lord, you would not have honoured my household with your presence."

Hugh flung his goblet of wine from the table and stood up. "I'm for bed," he announced. "See that my boots are cleaned by the morrow. We leave early."

After he left, King Edward spoke. "I thank you for your welcome," he said humbly to his host. "You have fed us and sheltered us, and I am in your debt." Before retiring, he chose five men in whom he had the utmost trust to meet with him privately; among them were his nephew and two squires.

"I would send a message to the queen and my eldest son," he told them. "Inform Her Grace that I would discuss with them diverse affairs affecting the realm." It was not a capitulation, but it was an acknowledgment of the shifting roles in which he and his family found themselves.

The next morning, they left at sunrise. Edward noticed that there were several faces missing from the gathering of his servants. He was not surprised; the desertions were not new, and he supposed that each man now must look to his own resources.

As the king, Hugh, and the king's men continued on their journey, the grey clouds hanging sullenly above them opened up to release torrents of rain.

"We stop at Llantrisant!" Hugh yelled above the pounding noise of the storm, which had added thunder to the wild ballad of nature that was serenading the king's forces as they moved. "We'll take shelter there!"

Edward simply nodded. It didn't matter where they stopped; they had to get out of the storm.

As they neared the boundaries of Llantrisant, they heard the sound of horses approaching. It was not a day for travel; the storm was too violent and the deluge too powerful for casual riding. Hooves pounded the soil, which would soon turn to mud.

"Lancaster!" Edward called out in alarm, spotting the banner of his cousin.

"Ride!" Hugh shouted, putting his spurs to his horse.

They rode swiftly, but Henry of Lancaster travelled with a force of men who intended to achieve their ends.

Before very long, they found themselves surrounded by the advancing soldiers.

"Your Grace!" Henry of Lancaster called out, his voice carrying over the sounds of the storm and the noise of an assembly of armed men with weapons drawn.

Edward drew in his breath. "My lord," he replied, his voice equally emphatic. "You seek your king?"

The men drew apart to allow Lancaster to make his way to King Edward. "I am charged by the queen and Prince Edward to bring you with me to my castle at Monmouth," he said, his visor raised so that his eyes could meet the king's gaze.

"And what of me?" demanded Hugh. "I go where the king goes."

"Hugh Despenser, you are to be taken to Hereford," was the implacable response.

"You cannot order me!"

"I can, and I have an army to make you comply if you

should refuse," Lancaster replied.

"Edward, tell him—"

Henry of Lancaster, outraged by this disrespectful address of a subject to his king, moved closer. His face was set in a grim mask of controlled anger to conceal his sorrow at these proceedings. He cared nothing for the demise of Despenser, but to see Edward I's son reduced to this state of affairs was a tragedy. It was easy, therefore, to order Despenser to be bound and taken as a captive to meet his fate.

20 November 1326
Hereford, England
12:32PM

Hugh Despenser the Younger has been delivered to the power of the queen, who is based at the castle of Adam Orleton, the Bishop of Hereford.

Despenser arrived in disgrace, mounted upon an unimpressive horse, nothing like the destrier that a warrior would have ridden. Once they were out of sight of the king,

Lancaster's men had placed a mock crown of nettles upon Despenser's head; his servant, riding before him, carried his coat of arms reversed as a symbol of his defeat and disgrace. The crowds had lined up as news of Lancaster's triumph spread along the route.

They were in a celebratory mood, blowing upon horns as he rode by. They spat as he passed, and cheered the soldiers who had captured him. Despenser refused to look to either side, riding in his abasement with his eyes focused ahead of him, even though he knew that before him was his end.

"He should be tried in London," the queen said after Hugh Despenser and the guards had arrived and the prisoner had been securely confined. "His victims should be allowed to see him fall."

London deserved to see the hated favourite sentenced and executed. The crowded city was filled with supporters who would view Despenser's death as proof that God blessed the queen's success and that the prince was ordained to be crowned as their king. The city needed to be reclaimed from the madness that had overcome it after the mob took over, but the people also needed to be reminded that they were subjects and not masters.

For her part, the queen could barely restrain her excitement. Seeing the proud Despenser riding into the

151

castle grounds like a common felon, his disgraced coat of arms heralding his downfall, the crown of nettles piercing his skin and sending trickles of blood down his forehead, his arms tied behind him, sent a surge of emotion through her that was primitive in its force. All the humiliation that she had suffered through his engineering was exorcised. The lands that she had lost, the subjugation that she had endured, the displacement that she had suffered were suddenly minimised in light of this monumental event.

"Let him stew in his chains for a time," Mortimer advised her. "London will serve well as the place of his execution, but in the meantime, let him learn that his days are numbered."

23 November 1326
Hereford, England
3:12 PM

Despenser is a prisoner of the queen, who now represents the ruling authority of England, although Edward II is still alive and a prisoner at Henry of Lancaster's castle in Monmouth. Edward is well-treated by Lancaster, but Despenser enjoys no such solicitude in his cell.

Queen Isabella had not imagined the satisfaction she would feel at the Despensers capture.

He will die soon.

But first, he would suffer, and before he died, he would know that his own followers would go to their deaths as a precursor to what awaited him at the queen's hands.

In the meantime, she had much to do, and there were times in the succeeding days when she nearly forget about her prize captive. She was the queen, and she intended to be regent; in order to establish her qualifications for this role, she was determined to show herself as the authority.

There were papers to sign and announcements to make. Writs were signed regarding the king. The Great Seal was handed over to the bishop. In his wording, King Edward gave no indication that he was anything but willing to cede his power, writing that, with the wellbeing of his subjects in mind, it was his royal pleasure to send the Great Seal to Queen Isabella and Prince Edward.

Of course, this was not the reality. Edward hated Adam Orleton with a hostility that was entirely inappropriate since the cleric represented the Holy Church. When Isabella made this point, the lords agreed with her. In truth, many of them had been less than reverent in previous dealings with the clergy, but the construction of Edward's surrender must be carefully dealt with. He was still the king, at least for the moment.

Isabella was frowning over the wording of a response regarding the king, when the door to the room burst open and Mortimer charged in, followed by servants.

"Damn him! He's trying to cheat us of his rightful death!"

Queen Isabella, who was about to send for her son so that the prince could begin to take a role in the transition process that would transfer authority from the captured king to the waiting prince, looked up. "Who is cheating us?"

"Damned Despenser! He refuses to eat! He intends to die before we can kill him."

"That shall not happen! He will die as we have planned. Force him to eat!"

"We can not force him to eat. We must kill him sooner. There's no time to take him to London. We must try him immediately."

"Is he so close to dying?"

"Close enough," Mortimer said grimly. "What are these?"

"Papers to sign."

"That can wait. Despenser is first." Carefully, Mortimer pushed the papers to the side of the desk. He had not read them yet. "Summon the lords and let them know that the

154

trial will be tomorrow."

"Tomorrow? So soon?"

"What, you now long for him to live?" Mortimer asked sounding irritated.

"You know that I do not. I want him to die. He deserves death. But London is the place for this to happen."

"Would you put a corpse on trial merely so that it could be buried in London?" Mortimer asked curtly. "He must be tried tomorrow."

"Then he will die tomorrow." Isabella said with a nod. "But tonight, we rejoice. It's the Feast of All Saints," she added with a smile.

Mortimer returned her smile and drew her in his arms in a heated kiss. They were united in what, to others, might have seemed a blasphemous rallying of darkness and a perversion of holiness. But others did not understand the depth of the queen's suffering. Mortimer was her lover, and for all that he was an ambitious and avaricious man, he was her ally. They were joined together in a partnership that had been forged in hatred of the Despensers.

Now the end of their mutual enemy was in sight, but their passion remained.

24 November 1326
Hereford, England
1:32 PM

The lords are assembled for the trial of Hugh Despenser the Younger, who, in order to preserve the last vestiges of his dignity, has been denying himself nourishment in the hopes of dying before the queen's revenge can be enacted. But his hopes are denied by the sudden decision to try him without delay, and when he enters the chamber where he is to be judged, he is not a prepossessing sight, gaunt and wan from lack of food and drink, soiled with grime from his time in the cell, and clearly a defeated man.

Sir William Trussell was seated in the midst of the assembled lords, the elite of English nobility who were born to the responsibilities of their class and intended to see that justice, however gruesome, was done. Beside him was the queen.

Hugh Despenser, when he was brought in, saw Trussell, and his expression revealed that he knew that Trussell had been the agent of his father's execution. The repetition of the role was not a coincidence; Trussell was willing, and the queen was conscious of the fitness of the duplication.

The charges had been carefully compiled, and every

accusation that could be levied against Despenser was in place.

It no longer mattered if every charge was accurate or not, because Despenser's enemies had allies who were determined to see him pay for all his misdeeds.

Hugh Despenser the Younger had not only violated the lives of specific people, but he had imperilled the soul of England. England, in order to cleanse itself of his pollution, was required to vomit him from existence. The lords were ready to do their duty.

"Hugh Despenser, heed the words of your accusers. You are charged with the following:

The death of Thomas of Lancaster;

Piracy;

The imprisonment and murder of numerous magnates;

Exposing the queen to danger at Tynemouth;

Conducting yourself as a false Christian by robbing prelates of the Church;

Forcing the queen and the prince to escape to France for the safety of their lives;

Encouraging the king not to see the queen or the prince;

Causing the beheading of the greatest barons in the land;

Violence against Lady Barer until she was driven mad."

Not yet finished, Sir William went on.

"Hugh Despenser, you have been accused of committing vile and unnatural crimes against the queen.

"Hear now her words: '*I feel that marriage is a joining together of man and woman, maintaining the undivided habits of life, and that someone has come between my husband and myself, trying to break this bond. I protest that I will not return until this intruder is removed, but, discarding my marriage garment, shall assume the robes of widowhood and mourning until I am avenged of this Pharisee.*'"

Hugh Despenser made no reply. He was clearly weak, but he had heard the accusations made against him, and his jaw tightened in response. Yet that was the only evidence that he was cognisant of the proceedings.

"Withdraw, you traitor, tyrant, renegade, go to take your own justice, traitor, evil man, criminal!"

With that pronouncement, the trial adjourned to the place of execution. Despenser knew what was about to happen; he had seen others sentenced to the punishment before.

He was dragged by a quartet of horses through the streets

and brought to the gallows. Crowds gathered along the route, eager to witness his destruction in the name of justice.

The gallows was fifty feet in height, suitable in its morbid grandeur for a man who sought to rule a king, and ironic, as well. Despenser, who sought luxury and excess, could not have foreseen that he would begin the process of dying upon such a monumental structure.

The noose was fastened around his neck, but the hanging was incomplete as intended; he was made to suffer, but not to die. Not yet.

He was taken down from the gallows, panting from the hanging that had been meant only to strangle him, within an inch of his life, and from fear of what was to come. Were he the bravest in the land, he still would have quailed at what was about to happen.

Did he think of those he had sentenced as he now awaited the culmination of his doom? the queen wondered. Her eyes scanned the assembled barons. Roger Mortimer was with his peers, handsome as always, and intent upon the man who had been his enemy as well as hers.

Trussell called for a ladder, which was quickly delivered, demonstrating that the details of the trial had been planned well in advance. Two men bound Despenser to the ladder as a fire was lit.

"For your unnatural practices, and for alienating the affections of the king against the queen," Trussell continued, signalling to another man to come forward, "you shall suffer the removal of your manhood."

Realising what was about to happen, Despenser began to struggle against his bonds, but they had been tightly knotted, and there was no escape. The knife was quick, its wielder expert, and in full view of the barons, Despenser was castrated. His penis and testicles cut off mercilessly.

It was a customary sentence, but for Isabella, this grotesque violation of intimacy was recompense for the manner in which the favourite had stolen her husband from her bed. She thought that she could have performed the castration herself if there had not been someone present to do it.

It was an agonising process, and if Despenser had intended to remain stoic through his punishment, those aims were dashed as he cried out in pain, pleading with his judges to stop. He knew that his suffering was not yet done. He was eviscerated and his heart was cut off and thrown on to the fire. A judgment befitting a false-hearted traitor.

Even when he could no longer feel the physical sensations of torment, his desecration would continue.

His body was divided into four pieces, so that the sections

could be delivered to four of England's most prominent cities. The beheading was almost an anti-climax. As the bloodied head was raised and presented to the crowds, a cheer rose up. The people had been entertained by the gory spectacle. But they had also been privileged to witness the process of justice in its most visceral form.

The head would be taken to London so that all who looked upon it would know that the wages of sin had been paid as decreed. With his body in pieces and his heart no longer beating, the tormenter was gone from life. He would meet his God and would suffer the unending persecution of eternal flames.

The queen's eyes met Mortimer's, and he saw deep satisfaction in her gaze, as if what she had witnessed had finally calmed the rage that had burned in her heart.

That night, they would commemorate their victory in secret.

Mortimer was as good as his word that evening, boldly entering the queen's bedchamber through the secret passage, as if it were his right to do so.

Wearing only a royal, fur-lined robe, Isabella awaited her lover, her long, unadorned hair falling down her back as if she were a young girl.

Mortimer unfastened the lacings of the robe and cast it to

the floor. "*Ma belle*," he murmured in a reverent tribute to his appreciation for her beauty. "We have won."

"Both of them dead," she whispered as his kisses roamed across her body, setting fires of desire where his lips met her skin. "Dead."

Mortimer chuckled. "Quite dead, my beloved queen. Their stinking bodies will, alas, taint the sacred soil of England, but such is the just fate of those who violate the sanctity of royalty. We have triumphed, Isabella, and England is ours."

England would be her son's, Isabella thought as she gave in to the ownership of Mortimer's lovemaking. That was what he had meant, of course, even though he had not identified Edward among the winners.

But her thoughts were soon focused only on Roger Mortimer and the salvation she had found in his arms.

30 November 1326
Monmouth Castle, Wales
09:42 AM

He is still the king, but for Edward II, his rule is over. He is

a prisoner in the castle of his cousin, Henry of Lancaster.
Hugh is dead. The queen and her lover Mortimer represent
the ruling authority in England, but Edward knows that as
long as he is alive, he is an obstacle. He is fatalistic about
his future. What becomes of a superfluous king? He knows
the history of his land, but there is no precedent for what
has transpired.

Isabella had had her revenge. No one bothered to spare
Edward the recounting of what had happened to Hugh, nor
had they skimped on the details. Even his cousin, Henry of
Lancaster, in whose custody he was held, had been blunt.

No one, it seemed, could honour the bonds of love that
he had felt for Hugh. Everyone, determined to punish him
for that love, sought to make him a witness to the event,
until his head was crammed with the vile images of Hugh's
agony.

The door to his room opened. Although he was not in
chains, or imprisoned in a cell, his chamber was under
constant guard, and there was no mistaking his status. He
was fed and clothed, and his needs were attended to, but he
was a prisoner.

"My lord." Edward remained seated as he greeted his
cousin. He was the king, and he did not rise for lesser men.

Henry gestured towards the chair across from the king,

and Edward inclined his head. It was a ruse; his cousin could have sat down at any time without permission, but he appreciated the trappings of respect, even if they no longer had any foundation.

"In time, Your Grace, we must decide what the future has in store for us."

Edward gave a mirthless laugh. "I have no future, Cousin Lancaster. I am a doomed man. I am but a kingly obstacle."

Lancaster did not assuage the king with meaningless promises that could not be kept. He was a realist with a glimpse of the future that exceeded the perspective of the king in his cell and the queen in her bedchamber. Henry looked to Edward the prince. "Your son," he said. Edward was still a father. "He will rule England."

"The time will come when you will need to decide to formally how your reign will...conclude," Lancaster went on. "It is too soon, just yet, for the lords to decide how to proceed."

"The lords to decide?" Edward repeated in a mocking voice. "It would seem, then, that you are all intent on treason. My son is the heir, and my son shall rule England, not a horde of nobles intent upon climbing over one another on their way to the throne."

"How matters proceed depends upon you," Lancaster said.

"How is that? Have you come for a royal audience? Do

you seek my favour? Do you seek a boon? I hear that you have reclaimed your title."

"It is mine by right," Lancaster returned. "But I did not come here to speak of my title."

"Do you seek another title? The title of king?"

"I seek to serve King Edward III," Lancaster replied deliberately.

Edward said nothing. He gazed into the fire; it was a cold day in late November. Advent had begun, the season of waiting for the birth of the Saviour. Edward knew that there was no saviour, human or divine, for him.

At last, the king spoke.

"Edward III. My father died knowing that I would succeed him. I grew up as the heir. His death was nonetheless a shock, but I was ready to be king. Perhaps you forget."

"I do not forget, Your Grace."

"My son." The third Edward. How would he reign? He was a boy. He clenched his fists.

"Mortimer will seek to rule through my son. The queen is besotted and will not see it."

"I will look out for my king."

"What will you do?"

"I will do my duty to the royal family."

Well at least I can rest assured Isabella will ripped anyone who dares lay a hand on our son, Edward thought. He could fault her for much, but in this she had to be praised. The she-wolf would protect her own, fiercely.

His gaze returned to his cousin. They were dancing around the subject, and Edward knew it. Yet he could not put into words what Lancaster wanted to hear.

"A fine example of loyalty you set," Edward accused him of instead. "I am a prisoner in your castle, denied my freedom and denied my place."

"Queen Isabella has made the same charge against you. You chose Despenser over your queen. It's been said that you wished her physical harm."

"That is a lie!"

"It has been said that you intended to strangle the queen and the prince."

Edward was aghast. "God knows I thought it never." Grief overcame him. "I would I were dead. Then would all my sorrow pass."

"You are not dead. You have a duty to your son."

"Tell me what you want, cousin."

"After the Christmas season, decisions will be made. The country must have a king. It must be your son. But how to manage this?"

"Why ask me? To feign as though my views matter is to mock me, cousin. What do you want?"

"I come to you now, in private. What is discussed between us remains within these walls, where there is no one to hear. But I will come again, after the season ends, with a proposal. If you abdicate as king, your son can be crowned. If you refuse to give up the throne, I cannot ensure that the prince will take the throne as Edward III."

Edward, burdened by the proposal that his cousin presented, covered his face with his hands and moaned.

"I am king," he cried out. "And my son will be king after me."

"There cannot be two kings, Your Grace. I do not ask for your answer now. But in January, I will return to you, and then I will need your answer. I pray that when you answer, you will do so with your son and England in mind."

30 November 1326
Hereford, England
11:18 AM

The month that has been bathed in bloodshed is coming to an end. The season of Christmas, the time of the Prince of Peace, is about to begin. For the queen, the uncertainty of the preceding months has given way to a glorious triumph, and in her company, the prince maintains a façade of pleasure at the success of her efforts. In private, however, he recognises complications that must be resolved if he is to know any serenity along the path his future is destined to follow.

The hour was late. Prince Edward of Windsor dismissed his servants. They had left him, as he had requested, some ink and paper upon which to write. The flames in the fireplace provided warmth, and candles gave light. The castle was quiet. He was alone with his thoughts.

It was easier, he had found, to understand what he was thinking if he wrote the words down.

Dearest Philippa,

I hope that you are well. I think of you often. So much has happened since my mother and I left Hainault. I think often of our time together and the kindness of your father. When we are married, you will be the Queen of England.

Prince Edward paused. Would Philippa understand what he meant by those words? His father would not remain as king; his mother had told him as much, and his cousin Uncle Henry of Lancaster had said the same.

Neither had told him precisely how this was to happen, and Prince Edward did not know how to ask. He thought he could trust both of them, but everything had changed so rapidly that it was better not to put his questions into words. But what he wrote was true. Philippa would be queen. What role his mother would have, and what would become of his father, Prince Edward did not know.

I wish you were here, he continued to write. That was the truth. Philippa was honest and faithful, and he knew he could trust her. She would never engage in the sort of duplicity that had brought his mother to England at the head of an army.

His mother had done what was necessary, he knew that. He was not a fool, nor was he an infant.

His father had failed to serve the country as a king should do. His father had allowed royal favourites to dominate his reign…still he was his father and now he was prisoner at Uncle Henry Lancaster's castle.

When we are married, and we are king and queen, we will bring the holiness of wedlock back to the crown.

I will travel much as king. My grandfather was devoted to the queen, his wife and my grandmother, and she travelled with him everywhere he went. I want our marriage to be so.

I will follow my grandfather's ways. I have made a vow to

169

do this; you are the only one who knows that I have made this vow. My grandfather was a famous warrior, and I shall be the same.

I intend to claim France. I am the rightful heir, through my mother's line. My uncle Charles IV has daughters, but they cannot inherit the throne. I am the closest relative and the one with the most legitimate claim to the throne of France. I will seek the French crown so that I can honour both my grandfathers, Philip IV of France and Edward I of England's memories and my mother's heritage.

England must not be given cause to compare Edward III to his predecessor. Edward knew that he had to divide his loyalties towards his father; he was and would remain a devoted son, but when he was King of England, he could not allow himself to be subject to the flaws of those that came before him. He would take back what was rightfully his and restore honour to the throne

Did Philippa understand? Did anyone in Europe understand? His French aunts had been the scandal of the country for their adultery, and they had been punished for their sins. His mother's liaison with Roger Mortimer was no less a dishonour to the crown.

Why, Prince Edward asked himself silently, did royal parents dispossess themselves of the honour that the crown rightfully demanded? It was not necessary to behave as a monk; a man was a man, after all. Sins of the flesh were easily confessed.

He would be a man of whom the English would be proud, and he would have a wife who shunned the licentious vices of the flesh. Women were to be more virtuous than men, least the paternity of their children be in doubt.

I know that you will be an honourable queen. My grandmother was so, and King Edward I's second queen, my mother's aunt, was equally so. Queen Eleanor died, and Queen Marguerite retired to a convent, but they both upheld the honour of their station, and I shall depend upon you to do so, as well.

Did he sound as if he were scolding her? Or would sweet, honest Philippa understand how much he needed to have as his consort a queen who was the epitome of all that was faithful? In order to rule, a king was called upon to wield justice and mercy, to be a warrior and a peacemaker, to command the loyalty of his subjects, and their affection, as well. If he had any hope of succeeding in these dual obligations, he would need to have a queen at his side who was unfailing in her dedication to him.

I have seen much in these past weeks that often makes me doubt myself.

He paused. Should he admit that? Did a king ever concede his own weaknesses? He considered striking the words, but then decided to allow them to remain.

But I never doubt you. When we are old, you and I, and we think back upon these times, we shall remember that in the midst of calamity, we were united. We were faithful to our God and our duty. We will bring honour to England, for you shall be England's dear queen, and our subjects will cherish you as they cherished my grandmother, and I shall love you as my grandfather loved her.

I cannot promise that I will be a perfect husband or a perfect king. But I shall strive to be a king who serves England well, and to you, dear Philippa, I pledge my undying honour.

Prince Edward put down the pen. He did not know if he would send the letter to Philippa. Perhaps he would keep it to remind himself that he was about to undertake a sacred covenant with the people of England. The crown that would be placed upon his head would be a weighty reminder of his duty.

But he would not fail.

AUTHOR'S NOTE

THE AFFAIR

Isabella Capet proved to be an extraordinary woman. She did something that was unprecedented, no king of England have ever been removed from his throne before. Much less by a woman.

Whether or not she was romantically involved with her partner in crime, Roger Mortimer, is still a hotly debated subject. Clearly, to her contemporaries, there was no doubt. That said, there exists no clear evidence of any extramarital affair.

Furthermore, when the queen was finally unseated a couple of years later and Mortimer was charged and executed, none of the charges listed against him included adultery with the queen.

That said, whatever the nature of their relationship there is no question that somehow Mortimer had an undue influence upon the queen.

THE MURDER/DISAPPEARANCE OF EDWARD II

General speculation has it that Isabella was persuaded to turn a blind eye as her lover organised the death of her husband. However Isabella was never charged with the death of the king, neither by her son or by parliament.

What we know, is that, despite removing him from his throne, Isabella sent the king small gifts and letters throughout his incarceration in 1327 and appeared to care for his welfare. By Easter that year she informed parliament that she was ready and willing to visit him. They promptly forbade it.

A couple of month later, a messenger arrived with the news that the king had had a fatal accident. Edward III then immediately started sending out messages of this fact, without even waiting for a confirmation, which in itself was suspicious.

Edward II's body was allegedly buried at Gloucester Cathedral, with his heart being given to Isabella in a casket.

For many years after the funeral, there were rumours that the king had survived and was actually alive somewhere in

Europe.

With accounts of such people as William Melton, archbishop of York claiming that Edward was alive two years after he was supposed to be dead and the strange events of 1338, in which William Norwell described in the royal wardrobe account a man called *William le Galeys*, who "calls himself king of England and father to the current king." This William the Welshman was not executed for being a royal pretender but instead spent time with Edward III.

Whether or not Edward II died in 1327 or lived out his life in Wales is anybody's guess. His death/disappearance at Berkley Castle on 21 September 1327 remains a mystery.

THE POKER UP THE BUM

This has been a favourite rumour since the 14th century. Although many chronicles from that time make it clear that no-one actually knows how King Edward II died, this has been a long enduring story.

The story goes that a red-hot iron poker was inserted through a horn into the king's anus, burning his inner bowels and respiratory system leaving no outward signs of struggle.

However this particular story claims it took the weight of fifteen men to hold the king down and they suffocated him with heavy pillows first before subjecting him to the desecration. If he was already dead why in heavens name would they then put a red-hot iron poker up his bum?

Such tales have clearly been made up and perpetuated as a cautionary tale of the consequences of being a bad king who is a passive sexual partner with other men – after all, who wants to end up with a poker up their bum. No evidence has been found to support this theory.

THE EFFEMINATE KING

By all accounts, Edward II was not effeminate. He was tall and strong from all the vigorous outdoor activities he undertook.

Likely, he wasn't homosexual, but instead bisexual.

The love he felt for his queen and family was, without a doubt, real. This is evident in his reluctance to go to open war with his wife and son.

Furthermore during their 18 years of marriage on several occasions he intrusted Isabella with various responsibilities when he was away from his court. He trusted her.

As time moved on, it became clear he trusted his favourites and their comfort and presence more than his own queen's. It is clear from Isabella's own words that she felt that Hugh Despenser the Younger had stolen her husband from her.

WHAT HAPPENED NEXT?

Isabella and Mortimer ruled together for four years, with Isabella's period as regent marked by the acquisition of large sums of money and land.

When their political alliance with the Lancastrians began to disintegrate, Isabella continued to support Mortimer. He was subsequently overthrown by Isabella's son, Edward III, tried for treason, and executed.

Isabella was held in house arrest at Windsor Castle until 1332. She received frequent visits from her son and daughter in-law.

She lived a conventional luxurious life a as a dowager queen for the remainder of her days, and took the habit of the Poor Clares before she died on 22 August, 1358 at Hereford Castle, at the grand old age of sixty-three. Rumours that she lost her mind or went into mourning are nothing more than just that – rumours.

THE PRINCE OF WALES

Edward III is referred throughout the story as *Edward of Windsor*. His father Edward II, was the first "Prince of Wales", but he neglected to invest his eldest son, with that title.

The tradition of conferring the title of "*Prince of Wales*" to the heir apparent was revived by Edward III and continued by English monarchs ever since.

KEEP IN TOUCH

If you love Historical intrigue, be the first to find out about Georgiana Grier's historical releases:
https://forms.aweber.com/form/60/1465689060.htm
We will let you know as soon as they are available.

Georgiana Grier

Made in the USA
Columbia, SC
11 June 2017